Keeping Hearth and Home in Old OHIO

A Practical Primer for Daily Living

compiled and edited by
Carol Padgett, Ph.D.

MENASHA RIDGE PRESS
BIRMINGHAM ❖ ALABAMA

Copyright © 2001 by Carol Padgett
All rights reserved
Manufactured in the United States of America
Published by Menasha Ridge Press
Distributed by The Globe Pequot Press
First edition, first printing

Library of Congress Cataloging-in-Publication Data
is available from the Library of Congress
ISBN: 0-89732-420-X

Cover design by Grant M. Tatum
Text design by Grant M. Tatum and Annie Long

Menasha Ridge Press
P.O. Box 43673
Birmingham, AL 35243
(205) 322-0439
www.menasharidge.com

$\mathcal{F}$or

my mother
Dorothy Stiles Gillespie
1918–1995
who flavored her fare with inimitable flair

my grandmother
Myra McCord Stiles
1890–1967
*whose cornpones we still try to replicate
and whose life we still try to emulate*

my great-grandmother
Emma McCord
1851–1925
whose nineteenth-century recipes for living have made all the difference

Contents

Acknowledgments

Attempting to assign proper measure to those who assisted in preparing this nineteenth-century buffet reminds me of my grandmother's efforts to leave her family the legacy of her cornpones. We were wise enough to request her recipe while she was in her cornpone prime, and she was kind enough to comply. Of course, she had no recipe. Trying valiantly to render one, she tossed each ingredient into a bowl, retrieved it by handfuls and pinches, and noted its proper measure with care. But, alas, there is no measure for a cook's intuition or the size of her palm. Our family has never replicated Ma-Mam's cornpones. We continue, however, to be richly nourished by the spirit of the cook.

Though I have shaped *Keeping Hearth and Home* at a keyboard rather than a pastry board with ingredients pulled from library shelves rather than kitchen shelves, the process has been reminiscent of growing up in Ma-Mam's kitchen. Menasha Ridge Press Publisher Bob Sehlinger invited me to gather the ingredients for this bill of fare and—with grandfatherly patience far beyond his years—hoisted me to the mixing bowl and entrusted me with the stirring spoon. He and editor Holly Cross have welcomed my handfuls and pinches with enthusiasm, tended my spills with tact, and monitored my pace toward "getting dinner in the oven" on time. Associate Publisher Molly Merkle prepared simultaneously for the delivery of my first book and her first baby and has moved between kitchen and nursery to nurture both. Menasha editor Nathan Lott stepped in to gather ingredients when I needed to turn my attention to other gardens. Developmental Editor Carolyn Carroll, bless her heart, culled our gleanings and arranged the buffet table with impeccable taste. Designer Grant Tatum added all the right touches to make it picture perfect. And Tricia Parks brought to the table her marketing genius to expand our efforts from a neighborly dinner into a cottage industry.

Ann Nathews, Library Director of Southern Progress Corporation, with the generosity of a neighbor offering a "starter batch," enriched our garden of ingredients with literary fodder stored in corporate silos. Sipping tea with a friend who approaches large gardens with aplomb was a fine way to ease into a daunting task! My husband Ben encouraged me to accept Bob's invitation by donning an apron, offering his personal and technological support, and purchasing a hand-held scanner. He has been a faithful "useful man" . . . literally "taking care of the vestibule steps, the sidewalk and the porch area" because it makes me smile at the end of a long day. From the other end of our marital computer table, he has added the secret ingredients of per-spective and humor.

The staff at The Western Reserve Historical Society Archives/ Library and the Jerome Library Center for Archival Collections at Bowling Green State University provided valuable information about Ohio cooks of 100 years ago. Ohio native and Alabama colleague Kelly Snow Preston and her grandmother Edna Chapman of Wooster de-voted a rare weekend together to on-site research in the Clark and Wayne County Libraries. And Paul Resetar, manager of the Golden Lamb in Lebanon, generously provided authentic Shaker recipes served since the nineteenth century in Ohio's oldest inn.

Ohio women of the nineteenth century have been my companions and mentors. Their recipes and "receipts," mores and maxims provide glimpses into the principles with which they nourished their relation-ships and the practices by which they ordered their everyday lives. More than anything, their quaint language has stirred my heart; and our hearthside conversations have seasoned my soul. As one of our nineteenth-century forebears said upon presenting a similar book: "I have enjoyed the task heartily, and from first to last the persuasion has never left me that I was engaged in a good cause."

Introduction

For what have Ohio women been conspicuous? The answer is a simple one—Ohio women never were and are not now "conspicuous." To be conspicuous has never been thought by them desirable. They have written; have sung; have moulded in clay; have carved in stone; have had place and power; but forward, notorious, conspicuous in the common sense they have never been. In this their inheritance is revealed.

> —An Ohio centennial speech entitled
> "The Part Taken by Women in the
> History and Development of Ohio," delivered
> by Mrs. James R. Hopley on May 20, 1903,
> Columbus, Ohio

This book is a lovingly constructed anthology of homemaking advice culled from a wealth of mid- to late-nineteenth-century cookbooks, household manuals, and periodicals. It is, in essence, a greatest-hits album of the domestic wisdom of the time, a simpler time, a time (for most Ohians) without electricity, telephones, automobiles, supermarkets, and countless other conveniences we take for granted today. My passion for capturing the wisdom of this age resides in my lifelong fascination with the everyday lives of those who came before me: What was it like to live then? What were the tasks and pleasures that filled the hours of each day? I have always treasured the old-time literature of the home as a tender personal keepsake, much like the legacy of handwritten recipes and hand-stitched finery that my female predecessors left behind. For me, putting this book together was an opportunity to step into the shoes of my great grandmother, or even of her mother. I can see them sitting side by side, skimming these pages in search of just the right recipe for calf tongue, a trustworthy treatment for a colicky infant, or the best advice for making fine cologne water in anticipation of a rare night out.

I smiled and chuckled my way through the work of choosing the most representative pieces of advice to include. My mother, grandmothers, and all the great aunts, bedecked in their finest aprons and best memories, gathered in spirit 'round the hearth of my desk to help select and stir ingredients. We laughed at the measures and manners of yesteryear and lampooned the family legends of which we were reminded. Simultaneously 57 and seven, I rejoiced in the reverie of the childhood Sunday dinners that nourished our family with home-cooked food and touchstones of predictability—forks on the left, hands in the lap, elbows off the table, and my grandfather's weekly admonition to "count the silverware before taking out the trash." From the vantage point of my fifth decade, I relived my first: lips puckered to be glossed for a trip to town, eyes wide in search of "ladies" (who "could be spotted a block away by the presence of gloves"). Seventeen once more, I revisited reminders familiar to women of earlier eras: "It is just as easy to love a rich man as a poor man" or "Every young woman needs an education and skills to fall back on *just in case*."

It is my hope that *Keeping Hearth and Home* will stir your memories and bring the lives of your great or great-great grandmothers into the storytelling circle beside your family hearth, for this is how they lived; and this book is one they might have consulted, had such a comprehensive collection been available during their day. Instead, our forbearers consulted a variety of sources, learning about household management from receipts in the addenda of period cookbooks and learning the finer points of proper deportment and social propriety in the designated columns of weekly newspapers and in magazines such as *Godey's Lady's Book, Harper's Bazaar,* and *The Ladies Repository.*

These texts connected women to the broader society and assisted them in examining and shaping their individual lives. In fact, this literature became so extensive that *The Enterprising Housekeeper,* written in 1897, noted that it was "almost the fashion to apologize for taxing a much-abused public with the burden of a new book on this subject." Yet how grateful we should be for the abundance of this literature to educate us about the lives of our ancestors. How I have been humbled by this nineteenth-century wisdom, for so much of which our twentieth and twenty-first centuries have claimed credit. It seems, more accurately, that women through the ages have agreed on a number of basic principles for orchestrating a home, harmonizing a marriage, and fine-tuning the children. As you shake your head at the quaintness of one practice—*A married gentleman shows respect for his wife by speaking of her as 'Mrs.' and never as 'my wife'*—or feel your skin prickle at the ignorance of outmoded mores—*A lady is at her best when she exhibits a modest and retiring manner*—you will also, surprisingly, often marvel at the modern-day wisdom of other instructions—*Better to live in one room, with all the furniture your own, than occupy a whole house with scarcely a chair or a table paid for.*

I tried to present the information in this book in the order in which it might have been required by a young Ohio woman around the turn of the century, from the time when she had reached early adulthood but was still living in her father's home, to the time when she was establishing her own household as a newlywed, to the time when she was preparing her own children to leave home and enter the world.

And speaking of the world, what was taking place there? In the 1870s, light shone on Ohio when Milan's Thomas Edison invented the incandescent light bulb, as well as the phonograph and early motion picture camera, and Charles Brush installed arc streetlights to make Cleveland America's first electrically lighted city. In the 1890s, John Lambert of Ohio City made America's first automobile, and Henry Timken of Canton developed the roller bearing. A temperance organization formed in Oberlin in 1893 became the nucleus of the Anti-Saloon League of America. Shouting "the saloon must go," its members led a moral crusade that resulted in a Constitutional amendment. Yet amid the commotion of commerce and the concerns of community, the nineteenth-century home was a ship in safe harbor with a woman at the helm, and it was advice such as that preserved here that guided her work on deck.

If she shall thus succeed in disseminating a knowledge of the practice of the *most suitable system of domestic art known in our country*;

if she shall succeed in lightening the labors of the house-wife by placing in her reach a guide which will be found *always trusty and reliable*;

if she shall thus make her tasks lighter and home-life sweeter;

if she shall succeed in contributing something to the health of American children by instructing their mothers in the art of preparing light and wholesome and palatable food;

if she, above all, shall succeed in making American homes more attractive to American husbands, and spare them a resort to hotels and saloons for those simple luxuries which their wives know not how to provide;

if she shall thus add to the comfort, to the health and happy contentment of these, she will have proved in some measure a public benefactor, and will feel amply repaid for all the labor her work has cost.

—Marion Cabell Tyree
granddaughter of Patrick Henry
Lynchburg, Virginia, January 1877

PART ONE

While Still in Your Father's Home

CHAPTER ONE

*D*EVELOPING THE MANNERISMS OF A LADY

Young ladies, while still in your father's home, waste not the time. Take the opportunity to refine yourself in every conceivable way.

*D*eveloping Usefulness and a *S*ense of *S*elf Worth

DEPEND ON YOURSELF. Young ladies from 17 upwards begin to ponder anxiously what to do next with their lives. Girls finish their education, come home, and stay at home. They have literally nothing to do, except to fall in love; which they accordingly do, as fast as ever they can. Many think they are in love when in fact they are only idle.

BEWARE MATRIMONY FOR ITS OWN SAKE. If you find yourselves searching not for the man, but for any man who will snatch you out of the dullness of your lives, find instead your own occupations and marry only the man with whom you may truly make a happy home. No matter marriage or work, young ladies must practice self-dependence.

CONSIDER YOURSELF AN EQUAL. The age of chivalry, with all its benefits and harmfulness, is gone by for us women. We cannot now have men for our knights-errant, expending blood and life for our sake, while we have nothing to do but sit idle on balconies and drop flowers on half-dead victors at tilt and tourney. Nor, on the other hand, are we dressed-up dolls, pretty playthings, to be fought and scrambled for. Life is much more equally divided between us and them. We are neither goddesses nor slaves; they are neither heroes nor semi-demons—we just plod on together, men and women alike on the same road.

Developing Good Habits for Personal Appearance

BE TIDY. Young girls, don't allow yourselves to fall into untidy habits. There is nothing more displeasing than an untidy woman, old or young. Hair full of dust, shoe buttons pinned on, nails with black rims, clothes ill-fitting, basted, and pinned. In fact, there is no limit to the untidiness that a person will fall into who is given to this sort of thing. Be neat and cleanly, both in mind and body. If you have not an inherent love of cleanliness, cultivate it.

STOCK YOUR TOILET. No matter how humble your room may be, there are eight things it should contain, namely: mirror, washstand, soap, towel, comb, hair-, nail-, and tooth-brushes. These are just as essential as your breakfast, before which you should make good use of them.

DON'T MIND THE COSMETICS. Just be as cheerful as you can. Make the best of things. Avoid disagreeable people. Don't read or listen to the horrible. Try to forget the unpleasant things in life. Be cheerful, be gentle, and so be lovely.

EAT WELL INSTEAD. Ladies who wish clear complexions, instead of using cosmetics eat vegetables and fruit as long as they are in season. And never throw away cucumber water or the juice of any fruit, but rub your face with it.

PRACTICE SMILES. There is a wonderful charm in a smile. Like charity, it hides a multitude of sins.

Laughter is day, and sobriety is night; a smile is the twilight that hovers gently between both, more bewitching than either.

—Henry Ward Beecher (1813–1887)
President, Ohio's Lane Theological Seminary

DRESS FOR THE DAY. Your everyday toilet is part of your character. A girl who looks like a "fury" or "sloven" in the morning is not to be trusted, however finely she may look in the evening. Never make your appearance in the morning without having dressed yourself neatly and completely after first bathing, if only with a sponge and quart of water, and caring for your hair.

DRESS FOR THE AFTERNOON. Make it a rule of your daily life to improve your toilet after dinner work is over and to "dress up" for the afternoon. A girl with fine sensibilities cannot help feeling embarrassed and awkward in a ragged and dirty dress and with her hair unkept should a neighbor come in. Moreover, your self-respect should demand the decent appareling of your body. You should make it a point to look as well as you can, even if you know nobody will see you but yourself.

ALWAYS DRESS SIMPLY. A true lady does not adopt gay and showy colors and load herself down with jewelry that is entirely out of place and conveys a very great anxiety to "show off." Custom sanctions more brilliant colors in dress goods than formerly, but they should be selected with modifications for outdoor wear; quiet, subdued shades give an air of refinement and never subject their wearer to unfavorable criticisms.

A DRESS SHOULD NEVER OVERPOWER THE WEARER. It should merely be an appropriate frame for a charming picture, bringing out the beauties of the picture but never distracting attention from it. So few women understand this. Your dress may, or need not, be anything better than calico; but, with a ribbon or flower or some bit of ornament, you can have an air of self-respect and satisfaction that invariably comes with being well dressed.

SELECT SIMPLE ACCESSORIES. Never carry coarse embroidered or laced handkerchiefs. Fine, plain ones are much more ladylike. Avoid open-worked stockings and very fancy slippers. For special occasions, fine, plain white hose and black kid slippers with only a strap of rosette in front are more becoming. Otherwise, wear thick-soled shoes, and in damp or raw weather always protect your limbs—either wear leggings or an extra pair of stocking legs put on before you put on the stockings.

SCENT YOUR ACCESSORIES NOT YOURSELF. Procure a quantity of poudres aux fleurs, fold it in an envelop so that it cannot escape, and lay it in the drawer appropriated to laces, gloves, and handkerchiefs, which will acquire from it that faint, scarce perceptible odor which is so pleasing. If a liquid be used, let it be as sparingly as possible. I only seek to impress upon my lady friends the truth of the old proverb as applied to perfumes: "Too much of a good thing is good for nothing." A handkerchief saturated with coarse eau de cologne or a strong essential oil marks at once a person as possessing very little good taste.

MEND CAREFULLY. If you have but three calico frocks, you can be as neat as if your wardrobe boasted of silk and satin gowns. Examine every garment when it comes from the wash and, if necessary, mend it with neatness and precision. Do not sew up the holes in your stockings, as we have seen some careless, untidy girls do, but take in a broad margin around the hole with a fine darning needle and darning cotton; cover the fracture with an interlaced stitch so close as to be strong as the body of the stocking and fine enough to be ornamental. Never let pins do duty as buttons or strings take the place of proper bands.

Developing Gentile Habits for Personal Carriage, Manners, and Speech

OCCUPY YOUR HANDS AND ARMS. A question often comes up, not so easily answered: What shall I do with my hands and arms? Some ladies carry a fan. But you cannot always have one in your hands, so it is better to practice keeping the arms pressed lightly against the sides in walking or sitting. This position, although a little stiff at first, will soon become easy and graceful. Ladies should never adopt the ungraceful habit of folding their arms or of placing them akimbo.

CULTIVATE YOUR MANNERS. A lady should be quiet in her manners, natural and unassuming in her language, careful to wound no one's feelings, but giving generously from the treasures of her pure mind to her friends. She should scorn no one openly but have a gentle pity for the unfortunate, the inferior, and the ignorant, at the same time carrying herself with innocence and single-heartedness that disarm ill nature and win respect and love from all. Such a lady is a model for her sex, the "bright particular star" on which men look with reverence.

GIVE YOURSELF OVER TO OTHERS:
* Do not fear to show that you have a heart.
* Do not hesitate to say a kind word to this one or perform a trifling act of courtesy for that one.
* Give a cheery word to the aged one whose journey is almost over.
* Speak the timely word to the sad-faced man or woman whose loneliness your well-meant effort will cheer.
* Do not be afraid to let the sunshine of your happy souls flow out and permeate all you meet.
* Be frank, easy, and cordial in your manners.
* Be cheerful and natural.

FIND YOUR MUSICAL VOICE. The sound of a discreet, well-modulated voice is a power in itself. Cultivate a low, clear tone of voice and an easy conversing manner free of gesticulation. Regular features cannot be cultivated. But a kindly expression can be cultivated and so, too, can a pleasant voice.

RESIST SLANG. The use of slang is becoming unbearable. Girls are unable to express themselves in standard language, and slang is growing more and more vulgar. It used to have the merit of a little wit, even if a poor kind, but now it is a meaningless jingle. And worse, it often carries a double meaning unknown to the speaker, which draws a smile, often of disgust, to the face of every man present.

CHAPTER TWO

*D*EVELOPING PRUDENT SOCIAL BEHAVIOR

Ladies, learn to comport yourselves respectfully outside the home, and you shall be respected wherever you go.

*P*rudence in *S*ocial *E*xchanges

DO NOT BOAST. In company, do not converse with another in a language that is not understood by the rest. If you chance to use a foreign phrase, don't translate it; it is equivalent to saying, "You don't know anything." Never correct the pronunciation of a person publicly, nor any inaccuracy that may be made in a statement. Boasting of wealth, family, or position is exceedingly silly and tiresome to the listeners.

LIMIT YOUR OBSERVATIONS. A quiet person is seldom disliked, while a noisy one sets the nerves all in motion and at war with each other. A noisy utterance is inefficient as disgusting. Noise, the disturber, deranges the mental faculties and incapacitates the mind for clear and deliberate thought. A boisterous, loud-talking man is disagreeable enough, but a woman who falls into the habit is almost unendurable.

BE NOT EXCESSIVELY FRANK. Do not take pride in offensively expressing yourself on every occasion under the impression that you will be admired for your frankness. Speaking one's mind is an extravagance, which has ruined many a person.

ALWAYS ACCEPT APOLOGIES. Only ungenerous minds will fail to do so. If one is due from you, make it unhesitatingly.

LISTEN. When a "tale of woe" is poured into your ears, even though you cannot sympathize, do not wound by appearing indifferent. True politeness decrees that you shall listen patiently and respond kindly.

LAUGH AT THE APPROPRIATE TIME. Don't laugh when a funny thing is being said, until the climax is reached. Do not laugh at your own wit; allow others to do that.

TAKE CARE HOW YOU GIVE ADVICE. The effectualness of giving advice will very much depend upon the spirit in which it is given. Blunt directness awakens and irritates our self-respect, while modest deference flatters us into self-unconsciousness. The absence or presence of a conciliatory manner is amply sufficient to account for the fact that the advice of some persons is almost uniformly an insult, while the counsels of others fall upon our perplexities like water-calming oil. Every look or tone that calls attention to the difference of the I and the Thou chills the atmosphere and causes advice to fall upon the soul as thumping hailstones; while a manner that covers this difference and evinces a tender unselfishness causes the words to distill on our hearts like evening dew. Manner is, in fact, almost omnipotent. Silken cords hold us fast where iron fetters would be snapped like gossamer.

DO NOT GOSSIP. A gossip is malicious and uncultivated; if nothing worse, she is empty headed. Do not hold up the peculiarities of absent friends to ridicule or discuss them uncharitably. Never speak disparagingly of another or rejoice in another's misfortune—it will be charged to envy. News that is not well vouched for should not be repeated—else you may acquire the reputation of being unreliable.

REFRAIN FROM INTERMEDDLING AND PRYING. Do not ask about the private affairs of anyone, such as what caused them to leave their home and come to a strange country or city. Do not ask the age of another unless they are quite youthful, as some very sensible men and women are sensitive on this point; whether it be considered silly or not, they have a right to keep their secret. To look over the shoulder of another is rude, as in the common fashion of looking over a newspaper, which a neighbor in the streetcar is reading.

REFRAIN FROM EYEING OVER OTHER WOMEN. The eyeing of women by women is one of the most offensive manifestations of superciliousness within society. Few observant persons can have failed to notice the manner in which one woman, who is not perfectly well-bred or perfectly kind-hearted, will eye over another woman whom she thinks is not in such good society and, above all, not in so costly a dress as she herself. Who cannot recall hundreds of instances of that sweep of the eye, which takes in a glance the whole woman and what she has on from top-knot to shoe-tie. It is done in an instant. No other evidence than this eyeing is needed that a woman, whatever be her birth or breeding, has a small and vulgar soul.

REFRAIN FROM ABSORPTION WITH OTHERS' THOUGHTS. Such people fancy they can always rule better than their rulers, preach a great deal more appropriately and understand far better the wants of a congregation than their pastors, know incalculably better what other people should do with their money than they do themselves. Indeed, such are so absorbed with other people's thoughts that they have no thoughts left of their own.

DO NOT WORRY OVER SNUBBING. Do not delude yourself with the idea that you can please everybody. Always do that which is right, be diligent, do the most you can, pay no regard to the faultfinders, and you will find as many friends as any sensible person need desire. If people are offish and cool and determined to have nothing to do with you, let them have their way. In this business they are helpless; you hold the cards and can play them to suit yourself. They may shut themselves into the heart of an iceberg, but you can nose them out if you are a woman. And when you come to know them perfectly, how thankful you will be, in many cases, that they would not know you!

TREAT ENEMIES KINDLY. If you have an enemy and an opportunity occurs to benefit the person in matters great or small, do good service without hesitation. If you would know what it is to feel noble and strong within yourself, do this secretly and keep it secret. A person who can act thus, will soon feel at ease anywhere. If enemies meet at a friend's house, lay aside all appearance of animosity and meet on courteous terms.

BEWARE OF FAMILIARITY. Undue familiarity is evidence of coarseness. A lady should not permit a gentleman to remove a bracelet from her arm or a ring from her finger for the purpose of examination— she should take them off and hand them to him. A gentlemen should not place his arm on the back of a chair occupied by a lady. A married gentleman shows respect for his wife by speaking of her as "Mrs." and never as "my wife." Orders to servants should be given in a pleasant tone without a shade of familiarity.

KISS SPARINGLY. A greeting much in vogue in American families is kissing. This is a reprehensible custom and should not be tolerated in good society. The kiss is the seal of pure and earnest love and should never be exchanged save between nearest and dearest friends and relatives. Indeed, public sentiment and good taste decree that even among lovers it should not be so often indulged in as to cause any regret on the part of the lady should an engagement chance to be broken off. Let promiscuous kissing, then, be consigned to the tomb of oblivion.

BEWARE INAPPROPRIATE GIFTS. The only gifts which should pass between ladies and gentlemen who are not relatives are books, flowers, music, and confectionery. Flowers are the most unobjectionable and welcome of gifts. There is a delicacy in selecting an offering—whether of gratitude, kindness, or affection—that sometimes puzzles a considerate mind; where any such hesitancy occurs, we can turn to flowers with complacency.

Prudence on the Street and in Other Public Places: Ladies

WALK WITH CARE. A lady on the street should always walk in an easy, unassuming manner, neither looking to the right or to the left, nor walking too quickly. If anything in a store window attracts her notice she can stop and examine it with propriety and then resume her walk. In bowing on the street, a lady must merely incline her head gracefully and not her body. But she should always smile pleasantly. It lights up the features and adds a refreshing warmth to the greeting. Ladies do not chew gum on the streets.

GREET FRIENDS WITH DISCRETION:

- In meeting a number of friends together, do not make a difference in the warmth of your salutation; to meet one with reserve and formality and another with great effusiveness is ill bred.
- Ladies walking on the street are not expected to recognize friends on the other side of the road; to do so would necessitate habits of observation inconsistent with ladylike repose.
- A lady does not call out to friends or inquire after their health in a boisterous fashion.
- Ladies do not rush up to each other and kiss effusively. It is a foolish practice for ladies to kiss each other every time they meet, particularly on the street. It is positively vulgar; a refined woman shrinks from any act that makes her conspicuous. It belongs rather to the period of "gush" natural to very young girls and should be discouraged on physiological grounds, if no other.

ACCEPT ONLY APPROPRIATE GREETINGS FROM OTHERS. A lady is at her best when she exhibits a modest and retiring manner. No young lady will offer her hand with the same freedom as does a married or an elderly lady; the hand should never be extended to those who are not intimate friends. A lady should never permit one of the opposite sex to address her in a slangy fashion, touch her on the shoulder, or call her by her first name before strangers. No lady ever flirts on the street or allows a stranger to make her acquaintance—she may consider it only a bit of "fun," but she will surely not win the respect of that stranger and will also lose her own. A lady will not strike a gentleman with her handkerchief or tap him with her fan.

REGARDING CHURCH. Giggling, whispering, or staring about in church is a mark of ill-breeding. When discussing religion, a dispute is foolish—when there are 1.5 billion of people on the face of the earth speaking 3,034 tongues and possessing thousands of different religious beliefs, it is a hopeless task to harmonize them all. Take care also not to boast of your church work; a religion that ever suffices to govern people will never suffice to save them.

ON THE SIDEWALK. In passing people on the walk, turn to the right. Do not join forces with three or four others and take up the entire pathway, compelling everyone to turn out for you. Walk in couples when there are several friends in your party. Do not pass between two persons who are talking together.

ON THE STREETCAR. Do not introduce people in a public conveyance. It draws attention to a person and makes him unpleasantly conspicuous.

IN THE LECTURE ROOM. Whispering is impudent and interrupting a speaker is insulting.

WHILE IN SHOPS. Do not seize hold of a piece of goods, which another customer is examining, but wait until she has either made her purchase or passed it by.

IN HOTELS. Do not pass in or out of the general entrance of a hotel but by the ladies' entrance only.

ON TRAINS. An unescorted lady may make herself agreeable to her fellow passengers, if the journey be long, without being misconstrued; but an acquaintance begun on a railway train should end there. Very young ladies should be cautious and reserved with young men. A lady should try to arrange her trip, when without an escort, so that she will not be compelled to change cars in the night. If she has to do so, she must place herself under the care of the conductor or some married couple until the transfer is made. The reasons are obvious. There are always "wolves in sheep's clothing" who would direct her wrong, particularly in large cities. If she arrives in the place where she is to stop at night, and her friends have failed to meet her or may not know she is coming on that train, she had better not take a hack. Choose rather a streetcar, where there are plenty of people.

Ladies, learn the behavior indicative of a gentleman, and turn from those who behave otherwise.

Prudence on the Street and in Other Public Places: Gentlemen

BOW TO ALL YOU MEET. The manner in which a salutation is given marks the gentleman. In the country, and in small towns also, a very pleasant custom prevails of bowing to all whom you meet. It makes a stranger feel almost "at home." We bow to the old, the young, the rich, the poor, to our friends, and to those to whom we are indifferent. Each one of these salutes can be shaded so nicely that, to an observant eye, they have a distinct significance of their own. With friends of his own sex, a bow and a friendly word in passing are sufficient on the part of a gentleman.

GREET LADIES ONLY IF PROMPTED. A lady in the street, boulevard, or park may not be saluted by a gentleman unless he has received a slight bow from her; he may then raise his hat with the hand farthest from the person saluted, bow respectfully and pass on, not under any consideration pausing to speak unless the lady pauses in her promenade. If the lady friend is with another lady, he should include her in the salutation even though he is unacquainted with her. A gentleman must not presume upon such a chance introduction to a lady to call at her house or to walk with her when he meets her again. It is not obligatory upon a gentleman to remove his glove when shaking hands with a lady. If he chooses, he can say, "Excuse my glove," or he can observe a silence concerning it. A gentleman should not shake a lady's hand so violently as to annoy her, nor press it with such force that he will hurt her fingers.

GREET GENTLEMEN WITH DISCRETION. When gentlemen unaccompanied by ladies meet, each will raise their hat very slightly if they are on such terms as to warrant recognition, but they need not bow unless the person saluted is entitled to special marks of respect by reason of advanced years, social rank, attainments, or having taken holy orders. It is vulgar for a gentleman to greet a friend by slapping him on the back or playfully poking him in the ribs; no amount of intimacy makes it allowable. Likewise, nicknames are unknown in good society and should not be used in public. Do not be too familiar on short acquaintance nor presume to address new acquaintances by first name—this is a presumption which some people never forgive.

WALK WITH DISCRETION. Gentlemen will not swing their arms nor sway their bodies in an ungainly manner when walking; ladies are never guilty of any such ungraceful action and need no counsel in that respect. A gentleman never swaggers along the street shouting and laughing with his companions, his hat on one side, a cigar between his fingers, or switching a cane to the danger or discomfort of passersby.

DO NOT SMOKE AROUND LADIES. A gentleman should never smoke while walking with a lady, not even if she politely fibs by saying it is not offensive to her. He should not smoke where ladies are, under any circumstances. If he is smoking and passes a lady quite near, he removes the cigar from his mouth. Should a lady accost him on the street when he is smoking, he will at once extinguish his cigar and decline politely but firmly to resume it. Although there is no intentional disrespect in smoking, the act conveys the idea of slight regard for the lady.

WALK WHILE CONVERSING. When a gentleman meets a lady friend with whom he wishes to converse, he does not make her stand in the street, but walks with her a short distance until he has said what he desired to and then leaves her with a courteous bow.

REFRAIN FROM WHISTLES. On entering a public hallway or an elevator where ladies are waiting, a gentleman does not treat them to an exhibition of his skill in whistling. It is exceedingly impertinent and is a virtual ignoring of their presence.

HOLD OPEN DOORS; FOLLOW OR LEAD ON THE STAIRS. In passing through a door, the gentleman holds it open for the lady, even though he never saw her before. He also precedes the lady in ascending stairs and allows her to precede him in descending.

IN THE THEATRE. Loud thumping with canes and umbrellas in demonstration of applause is voted decidedly rude. Clapping the hands is quite as efficient and neither raises a dust to soil the dresses of the ladies nor a hubbub enough to deafen them.

Learning the Etiquette of Escorting: Guidelines for Ladies and Gentlemen

GENTLEMAN, ALLOW THE LADY TO SET THE COURSE AND PACE. When walking with a lady, the gentleman should find out before they start if she has any preference as to the route. He should accommodate himself to her pace.

GENTLEMAN, SET THE PATH. Gentlemen walking with a lady or with a gentleman venerable for years, attainments, or office will give the inner path to the person escorted, unless the outer portion of the walk is more safe. The concession will be made without remark, and the lady will assume whenever the gentleman changes his position that there is a sufficient reason for moving from one side to the other.

GENTLEMEN, OFFER ARM WITH DISCRETION. A gentleman, when walking with a lady in the daytime, does not offer her his arm, unless she is old or ill or he does so for the purpose of protecting her in a large crowd. If attending a lady in the evening, it is customary to offer her the arm. If he has the care of two ladies, he should give his arm to but one and they should both walk on the same side of him. It is a very amusing sight to see a gentleman walking between two ladies, a sort of a thorn-between-two-roses affair. When crossing the street with a lady who has his arm, the gentleman does not disengage his arm.

GENTLEMEN, CARRY MOST ARTICLES. When a gentleman is escorting any lady in any public place, it is his duty to insist modestly on carrying any article she may have in her hand. In this connection, permit us to say that a husband should always carry the baby.

LADIES, CARRY SOME ARTICLES. The parasol, when that is necessary as a sun shade, must not be borne by the gentleman unless, because of sickness or old age, the lady requires peculiar assistance. A lady at a ball should not burden a gentleman with her gloves, fan, and bouquet to hold while she dances, unless he is her husband or brother.

GENTLEMEN, HOLD THE UMBRELLA OVER THE LADY. A gentleman should not monopolize the umbrella when with two ladies in a rainstorm but should take the outside, holding it over both.

GENTLEMEN, ALLOW HER TO REST IF FATIGUED. During a walk in the country, ascending a hill, or walking on the bank of a stream, if the lady is fatigued and sits upon the ground, the gentleman does not seat himself by her but remains standing until she is rested sufficiently to proceed.

GENTLEMEN OFFER AND LADIES ACCEPT AID. The gentleman may assist a strange lady to cross if she is in need of such help. A lady may accept the assistance of a strange gentleman in crossing a muddy or crowded street; such attentions should be accepted in the spirit in which they are offered and acknowledged with thanks.

GENTLEMEN, ASSIST UNESCORTED WOMEN. If a gentleman sees a lady whom he does not know, unattended and needing assistance, he should offer his services to her at once. She will readily understand the gentle chivalry that prompts him and will feel that by accepting his kindness she does not place herself in a false light. When a gentleman goes to a ball without a lady, he must place himself at the disposal of the hostess and dance with any ladies she selects for him.

GENTLEMEN, DO NOT ASSIST ASCORTED WOMEN. A gentleman does not attempt to attend to the wants of a lady who already has an escort. It is a piece of impertinence to do so.

GENTLEMEN, OFFER AID WHEN ALIGHTING FROM A CARRIAGE. The gentleman should step out first and then turn and offer the lady both hands, particularly if the vehicle be some distance from the ground.

LADIES, ALLOW THE ESCORT TO ATTEND HIS DUTIES WHILE TRAVELING. When traveling with an escort, a lady should not concern herself with any of the details of her trip. It is presumed that he knows more about traveling than she does and it will annoy him to be continually asked about the safety of baggage, whether they are on the right train, and numberless other fussy questions that would scarcely be excusable in children. The lady or her relatives should supply the escort with sufficient money to defray all her expenses. Some prefer to have the gentleman attend to these matters and settle the account at the end of the journey, but a strict record of all the items should be kept in this case.

GENTLEMEN, ASSIST HER WHILE CYCLING. Of course, a gentleman who accompanies a lady is ever on the alert to assist his companion in every possible way. He will, of course, assist her in mounting and dismounting and, should she be so unfortunate as to take a header, he will soon be at her side to assist her to rise, making himself generally useful and incidentally agreeable. His place on the road is at her left, so that he may more carefully guard her when meeting other cyclers and teams, he risking all danger from collisions.

GENTLEMEN, DISMOUNT UPON MEETING FRIENDS. In meeting a party of cyclists who are acquaintances, if all desire to stop for a little conversation the gentlemen of the party dismount and sustain the ladies' wheels, the latter retaining their positions in the saddles.

CHAPTER THREE

CONSIDERING MARRIAGE

Most men and women find themselves moved by impulse and personal consideration to a favorable conclusion upon the subject of marriage. There are many, however, who—because they seek absolute personal perfection, are overcautious, are seeking for a fortune, or because of personal unchastity and uncleanness—decline to marry at all or hesitate until advancing life finds them the uncoveted possessors of single misery.

Selecting Your Mate

The essential requisites in a companion which are necessary to insure happiness and a life of devotion are to be found in strength of character, a healthy body, a judicious head, a loving heart, and these all brought into attune with a high and holy purpose in life.

SEEK DIVINE GUIDANCE. As marriage is a divine institution, no young man or young woman should enter into this relation without seeking divine wisdom and guidance. You should begin to pray very early, lest you mistake your inflamed amativeness for the leadings of divine Providence. Pray while your eyes are still open, for Cupid blinds many and then suffers them to be led to their ruin by lust.

PROCEED WITH CAUTION. If you are careful in the purchase of a horse, which you may dispose of if not found satisfactory, much more should you be judicious and call your caution into fullest exercise in the selection of one who is to be your life partner and from whom you can only be separated by death. Take time. Be judicious. Go slowly. If you rush into marriage with haste, you will probably spend the rest of your life in a perpetual penance. Be careful, lest the skeleton of horror steals into your life and enthrones itself where God designed that an angel of peace and blessing should preside.

LOOK BEFORE YOU LEAP. The frogs in Aesop's fable had a great fondness for water, but they were not disposed to leap into the well, because they could not get out again. But when we see the haste with which many young people rush into ill-advised marriages, it looks as if they had less sense than the frogs. Don't fall in love. Keep your affections, and your judgment, and yourself well in hand. Keep your feet under you. Take in the whole situation, and when you find yourself in love be sure you did not fall in.

LET LOVE AND REASON BE BLENDED. Reason is to love what a pair of spectacles is to a nearsighted man. Let your love be intelligent; mix your affection with brains. Reason enables the little fellow to look beyond the fair face, the sunny ringlets, the brilliant eye, the graceful form and features of his adored, beyond the festivities of the wedding and the beauties of the imagination, to the domestic fireside, to the kitchen comforts, to pudding, and the cash account. That's what reason conjoined with love will do!

BE EQUALLY YOKED. It is important that a husband and wife should not be unequally yoked together in any respect. Marry your equal rather than your inferior or superior. Where there is great disparity—either socially, intellectually, financially, religiously, or in any other respect—disappointment and unhappiness are like to be the result.

BE NOT DECEIVED BY FLATTERY. Few in the early period of life are insensible to flattery or deaf to the voice of adoration. Beware of the flatterer. Be not deceived by fair speeches. Be assured the man who wishes to render you vain of your outward charms has a mean opinion of your sense and mental qualifications. Remember, too, that a young girl vain of her beauty and whose chief study and employment is the decoration of her person is a most contemptible character.

CHOOSE A MAN ONLY SOMEWHAT FAMILIAR WITH WOMEN. A woman should avoid accepting a man who has been particularly successful with women. At the same time, she should look for one to whom woman is not an enigma, and who is a man of the world and of strong character, so that she may feel sure that when he chose her, he said to himself: "I know my mind. Happiness for me lies there." On that man she will be able to depend and lean safely.

STRAY FROM SPOILED MEN. A woman should avoid marrying a man who at home is the favourite of many sisters who constantly dance attendance on him. That man is spoiled for matrimony. He will require his wife to bestow on him all the attention he received from his sisters.

STRAY FROM THOSE TOO GOOD. I should advise you to shun a dragon of virtue like fire—she should prefer a dragon rather. A man may be good, but he must not overdo it. He who has no wickedness is too good for this world; not even a nun could endure him. Fancy, my dear lady, a man being shocked by you! The male prig is the abomination of the earth and should be the pet aversion of women.

CONSIDER SEXUAL COMPATIBILITY. Sometimes, even where a woman is endowed with fair physical powers and would make a helpful and congenial companion if she were equally mated, in her ignorance she consents to marry a man of great amative powers and insatiable sexual nature. The same is when a man, who is weak or of frail constitution, marries a woman of strong physical powers and dominant sexual nature whose sexual longings could be satisfied only by a man equally strong and of like tendencies. Such unions result in alienation and estrangement, and sometimes in unfaithfulness.

CONSIDER YOUR AGE. Marriage should not be unadvisedly or hastily entered into by young and immature persons, nor should it be unnecessarily deferred until the probabilities of a happy union are greatly diminished. Every community affords illustrations of misery, and some of murder, which are the result of the marriage of mere children or because of the union of the innocent and unsuspecting with those who have been notoriously vicious and corrupt. Late marriages have their own peculiar disadvantages. Each person in a marriage has to give something up, and each has to yield personal preferences for mutual benefits. This is more easily done in the earlier years.

DEFER IN CERTAIN CIRCUMSTANCES. It oftentimes happens that where a man is preparing himself for some great lifework, or finds it to be his duty to support dependent parents or invalid brothers or sisters, or where he is without a reasonable means of support for a wife, and for many other sufficient considerations, marriage may not only be properly but wisely deferred.

DON'T DEFER IN OTHERS. The mature man or woman, however, who defers marriage until he or she shall have acquired such an wealth as will enable him or her to live in splendor, or who prefers to live alone for the simple consideration of economy, will usually find that no amount of money and no possessions will ever be worthy of being compared with the blessings of married life, which he or she has missed.

CHOOSE LOVE OVER WEALTH. Prefer poverty and blessedness to money and misery. Better is a dinner of herbs where love is, than a stalled ox and hatred therewith. Be willing, if necessary, to start plainly and work for larger possibilities further on.

He is rich or poor according to what he is, not according to what he has.

—Henry Ward Beecher (1813–1887)
President, Ohio's Lane Theological Seminary

DO NOT MARRY ONLY FOR MONEY. Of the many evils of the present day, one of the greatest is marrying for money only. There is neither love nor reason in that. Avarice cannot succeed in acquiring riches in this way without receiving due punishment for its folly. Happiness cannot be bought with gold, and every person must be poor indeed in the absence of a small share of this indispensable requisite of the mind—happiness. However, money is no objection as a secondary consideration where true love is the prime and strongest object in marrying.

Riches are not an end of life, but an instrument of life.

—Henry Ward Beecher (1813–1887)
President, Ohio's Lane Theological Seminary

CULTIVATE YOUR TASTE FOR BOOKS. A taste for reading will always carry you to converse with men who will instruct you by their wisdom and charm you by their wit, who will soothe you when fretted and refresh you when weary, who will counsel you when perplexed and sympathize with you at all times.

LET YOUR ADVISERS BE FEW AND CAREFULLY CHOSEN. Even the more discerning and judicious are often mistaken respecting the health, disposition, character, and general capacity of those for whom an admiration has been awakened in their thought and fancy. It is often well to secure the opinion of some disinterested and sensible person who is well acquainted with the family history and who is also familiar with any eccentricities and peculiarities of the other party.

The Proposal

When the time for the proposal has come, your beloved might well consider these thoughts on how to proceed.

WHEN ASKING THE LADY. The mode in which the avowal of love should be made, must depend upon circumstances. The heart and the head—the best and truest partners—suggest the most proper fashion. Station, power, talent, wealth, complexion: all have much to do with the matter; they must all be taken into consideration in a formal request for a lady's hand. If the communication be made by letter, the utmost care should be taken that the proposal be clearly, simply, and honestly stated. Every allusion to the lady should be made with marked respect. Let it, however, be taken as a rule that an interview is best. But let it be remembered that all rules have exceptions.

WHEN ASKING HER PARENTS. When a gentleman is accepted by the lady of his choice, the next thing in order is to go at once to her parents for their approval. In presenting his suit to them he should remember that it is not from the sentimental but the practical side that they will regard the affair. Therefore, after describing the state of his affections in as calm a manner as possible, and perhaps hinting that their daughter is not indifferent to him, let him at once frankly, without waiting to be questioned, give an account of his pecuniary resources and his general prospects in life, in order that the parents may judge whether he can properly provide for a wife and possible family. A pertinent anecdote was recently going the rounds of the newspapers. A father asked a young man who had applied to him for his daughter's hand how much property he had. "None," he replied, but he was "chock full of days' work." The anecdote concluded by saying that he got the girl. And we believe all sensible fathers would sooner bestow their daughters upon industrious, energetic young men who are not afraid of days' work than upon idle loungers with a fortune at their command.

 PART TWO

New Husband, New Home

CHAPTER ONE

STRENGTHENING THE UNION

Newlyweds will heed these maxims if they have any hope of a happy union.

Rules for You Both

If you were not already my dearly beloved husband, I should certainly fall in love with you.

—Harriett Beecher Stowe
From a note to her husband of many years

TEND TO YOUR LOVE ABOVE ALL. If a man and a woman are to live together well, they must take the plant of love to the sunniest and securest place in their habitation. They must water it with tears of repentance or tears of joy; they must jealously remove the destroying insects and pluck off the dead leaves. And if they think they have any business in this life more pressing than the care and culture of the plant, they are undeserving of one another, and time's revenges will be swift and stern. Their love vows will echo in their lives like perjuries; the sight of their love letters in a forgotten drawer will affect them with shame and scorn; in the bitterness of their own disappointment they will charge God foolishly and think that every plant of love has a worm at the root because they neglected theirs, and every married life is wretched because they did not deserve happiness.

Love is the river of life in the world.

—Henry Ward Beecher (1813–1887)
President, Ohio's Lane Theological Seminary

WIFE, LEAN UPON HIM. Be neither vexed nor ashamed to depend on your husband. Let him be your dearest friend, your only confidant.

WIFE, ATTEND TO HIM. In matrimony, to retain happiness and make it last to the end, it is not a question for a woman to remain beautiful, it is a question for her to remain interesting. Love feeds on illusions, lives on trifles. Not the slightest detail should be beneath her notice in order to keep alive his attention. A rose on her head, her hair parted the other way, a newly-trimmed bonnet may revive in him the interest he felt the first time he met her, nay, the emotion he felt the first time he held her in his arms.

EXPECT WITHIN REASON. Hope not for constant harmony in the married state. The best husbands and wives are those who bear occasionally from each other sallies and ill humor with patient mildness. Be obliging, without putting great values on your favors. Hope not for a full return of tenderness.

CONFINE JEALOUSY AND RESPECT HIM. You need not be at pains to examine whether his rights be well founded. It is enough if they are established. Pray God to keep you from jealousy. The affections of a husband are never to be gained by complaints, reproaches, or sullen behavior. Respect your husband's prejudices. Do respect his relations, especially his mother; she is not the less his mother because she is your mother-in-law—she loved him before you did.

BE CHARITABLE, TOLERANT, AND HONEST:
- Never talk at one another, either alone or in company.
- Never both manifest anger at once—if one is angry, let the other part the lips to give a kiss.

- ☞ Never speak loudly to one another, unless the house is on fire.
- ☞ Never find fault unless it is perfectly certain that a fault has been committed, and even then prelude it with a kiss, and lovingly.
- ☞ Never taunt with a past mistake or reflect on a past action, which was done with a good motive and with the best judgment at the time.
- ☞ Never part without loving words to think of during absence— you may not meet again in life.
- ☞ Never deceive, for the heart once misled can never wholly trust again.

BE WORTHY OF TRUST AND DEFEND ONE ANOTHER. Once established in your home, preserve its affairs inviolate. You should have no friends save mutual ones, and those should never be made confidants of. Should any one presume to offer you advice with regard to your husband or seek to lessen him by insinuations, shun that person as you would a serpent. Whether present or absent, alone or in company, speak up for one another, cordially, earnestly, lovingly. A man or woman who will speak slightingly of a life companion has outraged the first principle of happiness in the marriage relation—respect and politeness—and is not fit to be trusted.

REGARD ONE ANOTHER SELFLESSLY. The very nearest approach to domestic felicity on earth is in the mutual cultivation of an absolute unselfishness. Let each one strive to yield oftenest to the wishes of the other. Neglect the whole world besides rather than one another. Never allow a request to be repeated; "I forgot" is never an acceptable excuse. Do not herald the sacrifices you make to each other's tastes, habits, or preferences. Let all your mutual accommodations be spontaneous, whole-souled, and free as air.

GIVE WITH CHEER. Tonics, stimulatives, medicines! There is nothing in all the pharmacopoeia half so inspiriting as a cheerful temper. Carry the radiance of your soul in your face. When you give, give with joy and smiling. Let your smiles be scattered like sunbeams on the just as well as on the unjust.

Consult One Another. If the poor house has any terrors for you, before you pay three cents for a jew's harp ascertain whether you can make just as pleasant a note by whistling, for which nature furnishes the machinery; and before you pay seventy-five dollars for a coat, find out first whether your lady would not be just as glad to see you in one that cost you half the money.

"*A*lmost two months married. The great step of life which makes or marks the whole after journey has been happily taken. The dear friend who is to share with me the joys and ills of our earthly being grows steadily nearer and dearer to me. A better wife I never hoped to have. Our little differences in points of taste or preference are readily adjusted, and judging by the past I do not see how our tender and affectionate relations can be disturbed by any jar. She bears with my 'innocent peculiarities' so kindly, so lovingly; is so studious in providing for my little wants; is, in short, so true a wife that I cannot think it possible that any shadow of disappointment will ever cloud the prospect—save only such calamities as are the common allotment of Providence to all. Let me strive to be as true to her as she is to me."

—Rutherford B. Hayes
Cincinnati
February 27, 1853

Own What You Have. It is too common for young housekeepers to begin where their mothers ended. Be satisfied to commence on a small scale. Better to live in one room, with all the furniture your own, than occupy a whole house with scarcely a chair or a table paid for. Abstain from frantic efforts to keep up appearances for which the price is paid in scrimping under the rose all the year round. Make your purchases with actual gold pieces and crisp bank notes from your pocket, so that you will see them visibly diminishing under your eye and the lessening heap will cry to you to stop. Eat and drink this month what you earned last month—not what you are going to earn next month.

Rules for the Husband

Ladies, expect from your husband that he should adhere to these guidelines for behavior to you, and let your sons learn by your insistence upon this behavior the considerate husbands they should become.

ACKNOWLEDGE YOUR WIFE AS RULER SUPREME. Whether or not it is best for kingdoms, in families the only safe form of government is autocracy. And the autocrat should decidedly be the lady, the mistress. A man has no business to meddle in the management of the house, no business to poke over the weekly bills and insist on knowing what candles are per pound, whether the washing is done at home or abroad, and what he is going to have each day for dinner. The master of the house has quite enough to do outdoors.

Women of Ohio must trace their type to . . . the first Puritan women who set foot upon [our country's] shores, for their ideals have persisted here, more or less distinct, surrounded but not yet submerged by many other types. This type, which produced women of independent thought, yet women who were home loving, not self-seeking, great mothers serving, but exacting honor and obedience, wives who were helpmates, not dictators nor dependents, was transplanted here. Today the women of this state are the conservators of the strong original type, and here, we believe, it is perpetuated with fewer of its earlier faults and more of its virtues than in any other state of the Union.

—Mrs. James R. Hopley
"The Part Taken by Women in the History and Development of Ohio," an Ohio centennial talk delivered in Chillicothe, Ohio, May 20, 1903

HUSBAND, SUBMIT. Unless you and your wife should prove to be different from all the rest of humanity, she will dominate and rule over you in spite of yourself; and you may as well recognize that fact and count upon it from the very beginning. If she is sweet and gentle, devoted and loving, she will hold sway and rule you by her loving devotion and womanly worth. If she is devoid of these good qualities, she will nevertheless rule you, but in such a spirit that you will be sure to recognize the fact that you are being driven contrary to your wish and judgment.

DO NOT INTERFERE OR FIND FAULT. He who voluntarily and habitually interferes in matters of the home must be a rather small-minded gentleman, uncommonly inconvenient to his family and, if present, to servants. Perhaps to more than they, since a man who is always "muddling about" at home is rarely a great acquisition to the world outside. A house where "papa" or the "boys" are always "pottering about," popping in and out at all hours, everlastingly wanting something, or finding fault with something else, is a considerable trial to even feminine patience.

TAKE YOUR WIFE AS YOUR HELPMATE. Husband, counsel with your wife and be assured light will flash upon your darkness. Woman is far more a seer and prophet than man if she is given a fair choice. If you are in any trouble or quandary tell your wife all about it at once. Ten to one her invention will solve your difficulty sooner than all your logic; what is wrong of your impulse or judgment, she will detect and set right with almost universally right instincts.

Self-expression and intellectual development were not retarded, because the home was recognized as woman's place and sphere, and largely because such ideals prevail in Ohio; the part taken by women in the history and development of the state has been important and far-reaching in its effect.

—Mrs. James R. Hopley
"The Part Taken by Women in the History and Development of Ohio," an Ohio centennial talk delivered in Chillicothe, Ohio, May 20, 1903

APPRECIATE HER. Praise your wife, man! For pity's sake, give her a little encouragement. It won't hurt her. She makes your home comfortable, your hearth bright and shining, your food agreeable—for pity's sake, tell her you thank her if nothing more. She doesn't expect it; it will make her eyes open wider than they have all these years, but it will do her good for all that, and you too.

The intelligence and moral force always associated with the women of Ohio, infused with their strongest trait—a bequest also from Pennsylvania and the South—a passionate devotion to home—are elements which constitute many an unrecorded but never obliterated chapter in the history and development of Ohio.

> —Mrs. James R. Hopley
> "The Part Taken by Women in the History and
> Development of Ohio," an Ohio centennial talk
> delivered in Chillicothe, Ohio, May 20, 1903

NOTICE HER LABORS. You know that if the floor is clean, manual labor has been performed to make it so. You know, if you can take from your drawer a clean shirt whenever you want it, that somebody's fingers have ached in the toil of making it so fresh. Everything that pleases the eye and the sense has been produced by constant work, much thought, great care, and untiring efforts, bodily and mental. It is not that many men do not appreciate these things and feel a glow of gratitude for the numberless attentions bestowed upon them in sickness and in health, but they don't come out with a hearty, "Why, how pleasant you make things look, wife!" or, "I am obliged to you for taking so much pains!"

BRING MANNERS HOME. You thank the tailor for giving you "fits;" you thank a man in a full streetcar who gives you a seat; you thank a young lady who moves along in the concert room. In short, you thank everything out of doors, because it is the custom. Then you come home, tip your chair back and your heels up, pull out the newspaper, grumble if your wife asks you to take the baby, scold if the fire has gone down; or, if everything is just right, you shut your mouth with a smack of satisfaction but never say, "I thank you."

BE ATTENTIVE. Command your wife's attention by being always attentive to her. Especially do not treat your wife with inattention when in company; it touches her pride, and she will not respect you more or love you better for it. If you would have a pleasant home and a cheerful wife, pass your evenings under your own roof.

BE AFFECTIONATE. I would rather see any affectionate girl remain an old maid for life than be made wretched by her union with a cold-hearted man. One reason why divorces are so common nowadays is because a want of love and praise on the part of husbands drives their once loving wives from their sacred home. Don't be so cold and distant, stern and silent in your own house while remarkable for sociability elsewhere.

AVOID PREACHING. Never take upon yourself to be a censor upon your wife's morals, nor read lectures to her, except affectionately. Let the good example be your preaching; practice virtue yourself to make her in love with it.

BE JUDICIOUS. Do not jest with your wife upon a subject in which there is danger of wounding her feelings; remember that she treasures every word that you utter. Do not entertain your wife with praising the beauty and accomplishments of other women. Do not speak of some virtue in another man's wife to remind your own of a fault. Choose well your male friends—have but few and be cautious of following their advice in all matters, particularly if inimical to the foregoing instructions.

MAKE HOME PLEASANT FOR HER. We hear a good many sermons nowadays that the chief duty of woman is to render home attractive to her husband. No doubt any good wife will make this her crowing pleasure; but where duty is in question, there is another phase of the matter which is sadly overlooked—the duty of the husband to make home pleasant for the wife. As a very small portion of his waking hours is spent in the house, where his wife's whole life is passed, it would seem quite as important that her convenience and tastes should be consulted first, for the sight of these things must delight or chafe her all day long.

RELIEVE HER BURDEN. The woman who takes care of the house has enough to do without choring after her liege lord or waiting on a lot of men all day. You expect her to keep the house neat and tidy. If it is not so, you run to a saloon. You expect her hair to be smooth, her dress in order, her stockings neat, your clothes in order, the dust kept from its thousand gathering places, something good to eat three times a day besides lunches, and herself to be as neat and attractive as she was the night you popped the question. How can she be all this, if she has to spend half her time picking up what you throw down?

THINK BEFORE ENTERING. Do ever men folks think how much work they make a woman by going into the house with muddy boots? It would take but a moment for them to use the scraper and leave outside the house the dirt, which they track over the floor, the oil-cloth, and carpet, or which they leave on the stove-hearth or fender—all of which must be mopped, cleaned, scraped, wiped, and scrubbed off.

THINK UPON ENTERING. You enter the door with a slam; it closes half, and some woman must shut it after you. Your overcoat is thrown on a chair in one corner; your hat sails away into another corner, to alight upon a stand or under it; gloves are thrown on a tableneck; wrapper hung on the first handy chair; and down you sit in the center of the room where everyone must navigate around you. For shame!

MAKE CEREMONY OF HER. Finally, I believe that men ought to spend most of their spare time in strewing with flowers the ground upon which a woman is about to tread.

It is recognized by alien as by native-born that for the West, Ohio has been the great civilizing center. [. . .] If Ohio is typical of civilization at its best, and, as Emerson said, "Civilization is the power of good women," then must Ohio owe more to the character of its women than many of its citizens have ever recognized.

> —Mrs. James R. Hopley
> "The Part Taken by Women in the History and
> Development of Ohio," an Ohio centennial talk
> delivered in Chillicothe, Ohio, May 20, 1903

CHAPTER TWO

SETTING UP HOUSEHOLD

Thoughts on Making the House a Family Home

CREATE AN ORDERLY HOME. The subject of house furnishing is more important than is often realized. The furniture and the decorations of a house and the condition of the house and grounds are an index to the character and closely related to the reputation of the occupants. Hence, neat, tasteful, and orderly homes, not necessarily expensive in their appointments, have a very important educational influence.

MAKE YOUR HOME A DESIRABLE PLACE. To beautify home is a duty we owe to that innate love of beauty which God has implanted in us. Adorn your house with books, pictures, papers, and enliven it with music. Plant trees for shade and for fruit, cultivate flowers and shrubbery, keep up the fences and keep the house painted. If a gate hinge or a door knob be broken, repair it at once; let nothing "go to rack." There is no folly in it, but the best wisdom. Your life will be happier and longer, and your children will grow up more refined and contented, cherishing a stronger affection for you and an attachment to the home that will make them cling to it and to you when old age comes on.

The greatest part of one's life is spent indoors, and the surroundings and decorations of our particular abode tend to make our existence either more pleasant or unpleasant, sober faced or mirthful in countenance, in degree, limited only by the temperamental organization of the subject.

—A. F. Fenstermaker, Decorator
Visitors Guide to Columbus, 1880

FOLLOW NATURE. Do not encourage shams—let everything be genuine. Do not paint wood to imitate bronze or plaster to look like stone. Remember that there is an eternal fitness in things. Comfort and taste can easily be combined. We may trust human nature to suggest the former; the latter is the fruit of unrecognized passing influences.

"The house of Elliott Jones & Co., at 6 Neil House Block, has the largest line of framed and unframed engravings in Central Ohio, a stock from which the most fastidious taste may be satisfied. The line is unsurpassed, consisting of line engravings, on white and India tinted papers; pictures in photo gravure; engravings colored in water colors by hand; velvet frames for card, cabinet and promenade photographs; passepartouts in great variety; easel frames of all styles; photographs of celebrities, photographic albums of their own importation; and pocket books, cigar cases, jewel cases, odor cases, lunch baskets, and fancy goods of all kind; and their specialties in West's Composition Statuary and Stoddart's musical library are worthy the attention of those desiring beautiful home decorations and good music at reasonable and cheap rates."

—"Shopping for Decorative Items in Columbus,"
Visitors Guide to Columbus, 1880

The Front Room

Let the front part of the house be thrown open and the most convenient room in it selected as the family room. Let its doors be ever open. When the work of the kitchen is completed, let mother and daughters be found there with their appropriate work. Even if the living room be plain, the children leave traces of their growing up in it, and the faces of the old people who have there lived their lives look down from its walls.

DRESS APPROPRIATELY. Let no hat ever be seen in that room on the head of its owner. Let no coatless individual be permitted to enter it. If father's head is bald—and some there are in that predicament—his daughter will be proud to see his temples covered by the neat and graceful silken cap that her hands have fashioned for him. If the coat he wears by day is too heavy for the evening, calicoes are cheap and so is cotton wadding. A few coins placed in that daughter's hand insure him the most comfortable wrapper in the world. And if his boots are hard and the nails cut mother's carpet, a bushel of wheat once in three years will keep him in slippers of the easiest kind.

OUTFIT THE ROOM WITH A READING AREA. Let that table, which has always stood under the looking glass, against the wall, be wheeled into the room, its leaves raised, and plenty of useful—not ornamental—books and periodicals be laid upon it. When evening comes, bring on the lights, and plenty of them, for sons and daughters—all who can—will be most willing students. They will read; they will learn; they will discuss the subjects of their studies with each other; and parents will often be quite as much instructed as their children.

TO PRESERVE BOOKS

"Bindings may be preserved from mildew by brushing them over with spirits of wine. A few drops of any perfumed oil will secure libraries from the consuming effects of mold and damp. Russia leather, which is perfumed with the tar of the birch-tree, never molds or sustains injury from damp."

—*Centennial Buckeye Cook Book,* 1876

DECORATE THE GENTLEMAN'S CHAIR. A pretty way to cover the upper part of the back of a chair is with a towel of fine quality and fringed ends. Tie the center of the towel with a ribbon or cord tightly so that the ends of the towel are left hanging like the ends of a necktie. Put the tied center of the towel in the middle of the back of the chair and spread the ends out, putting a bow of ribbon at the center where the towel is tied. This is particularly tidy for a gentleman's high-backed chair, as he may lean his head on either side without soiling the chair.

DECORATE THE ROCKING CHAIR. The ugly back of a splint rocking chair can be improved by covering it with a strip of drab linen with a narrow border in outline stitch on each edge. Slip one end between the strips of wood at the top and bring the other end under at the bottom and fasten them securely. They may be kept in place by tying them to the rounds at the top. If done with ribbons, this looks pretty.

DECORATE THE WALLS EASILY. The cover designs and full-page illustrations of several of the leading monthly and other periodicals are reproductions of the best works of prominent artists and illustrators. These are freely used in many homes to decorate the walls of libraries, dens, and sometimes living rooms, either framed or bound in passepartout binding or merely neatly trimmed with a straight-edge and attached to the wall by means of brass-headed tacks or thumb tacks. A series of cover designs of one or more periodicals makes a very interesting and attractive frieze for the den or library.

Some people can be happy when occupying an apartment entirely devoid of artistic embellishment. But no one will deny that the same person will see brighter charms in life's pilgrimage if surrounded by artistic adornments in place of the barren walls.

—A. F. Fenstermaker, Decorator
Visitors Guide to Columbus, 1880

"In forming and adapting all the most tastely designs of the present styles of wallpapers, to the various apartments of a residence, and their juxtaposition with the furnishing and purposes of the respective rooms, and finally, in arranging the selected ornamentations, Mr. Fenstermaker has no superior in Central Ohio. The large extent of his business, the numerous first-class artists employed by him in the different departments of Frescoeing, Painting, Paper Hanging and Kalsomiming, must surely convince us that this gentleman conducts his business to the entire satisfaction of a large patronage. His location and address is 102 E. Town St., Columbus, Ohio. Designs and estimates furnished upon application."

—A. F. Fenstermaker, Decorator
Visitors Guide to Columbus, 1880

The Dining Room

Of all rooms in the house, the dining room should be the cheeriest, because it is there that all members of the family are most likely to congregate. No matter how widely the interests and occupations of father, mother, and children may separate them at other times of the day, at least one fifth of their waking hours will probably be spent at the table.

In fitting the dining room, its capacities should be studied. Unless there is ample space, no superfluous ornamentation should be attempted: all desirable room should be given to the necessary furniture. Here, a list of furniture recommended:

TABLE. The table should be firm and solid and not so shaky that the guests fear some catastrophe. Decidedly, square and round tables are the most desirable, because, placed in a circle or nearly facing the host, no guest is given precedence except those who occupy the seats of honor at the right hand of the host and hostess respectively.

CHAIRS. Chairs upholstered with leather are the nicest, and oak chairs with high backs are popular. Chairs can be made absolutely comfortable with practicable cushions; small hassocks can be placed under the table for additional comfort. Cane-seat chairs should never be used in the dining room—they catch beads and fringes and play sad havoc with them. The perforated wood ones are equally bad—the brass-headed nails with which they are fastened catch worse than the cane, and many a delicate fabric has been ruined by them.

SERVING TABLES. A side table for carving will be needed. This carving table can be mounted on rollers so that it can be brought near the dining table when it is required. The sideboard may be of any fancied design which affords the convenience of shelves for plate and table ornaments, and drawers and undercloset for linen, cutlery, plate, and fine glassware. The drawers used for plates and the under-closets should be provided with locks.

CHINA CLOSET. The china cabinet is a useful and beautiful article of furniture, but in the absence of such a cabinet any ordinary closet opening into dining room may be utilized by replacing its door with a decorative door with diamond panes of glass or with a drapery hanging from a rod and drawn aside when the dining room is in use.

LOOKING GLASS. When a looking glass or mirror is used, either as part of a sideboard or for wall decoration, care should be taken that no rays of sunlight strike it; their chemical action destroys the perfect distribution of the amalgam with which the reverse of the glass is coated and causes an appearance of granulation or crystallization upon the surface of the mirror.

INSTALL AMPLE SOURCES OF WELL-PLACED LIGHT. The ideal dining room is bright with sunlight or lamplight. If it is possible to admit sunshine to the dining room, it should be done. In the country, enjoy the delight of an outdoor dining room upon the piazza or lawn. In cities, dependence must be placed upon neutral-tinted walls and draperies, enlivened by freshly colored pictures, the light of open fires, and the soft colors of candle flame and shaded lamps. If there can be only one open fire in the house, put it in the dining room. The lighting of a dinner table is of importance. The pleasantest light falls from candles or lamps, which should be so placed as not to incommode the diners. Lamps are sometimes suspended over the table, as are gas fixtures. Side lights are apt to cross the light so that it is unpleasant; if they are used, they should be shaded.

Good oil poured in a teacup or on the floor does not easily take fire when a light is brought in contact with it. Poor oil will instantly ignite under the same circumstances, and, hence, the breaking of a lamp filled with poor oil is always attended by a great peril of conflagration [. . .] Good kerosene should be clear in color and free from all matters which gum up the wick . . .

—Catherine Beecher and Harriet Beecher Stowe
*The American Woman's Home or Principles of
Domestic Science,* 1869

WALLS. Many dining rooms are furnished with dark wood; the walls are gloomy or covered with dismal pictures of dead game and fish. Instead, let the pictures be of fruit or of other still life with bright colors. The most modest establishment admits these possibilities, and from them the plainest repast gains a charm.

FLOOR. The floor may be bare. Indeed, a wooden floor with one or more rugs is preferable to a carpeted floor. Woolen fabrics attract and retain odors, especially those arising from heated fat. For this reason, as well as upon the score of cleanliness, a movable carpet or rug is better for dining-room use than one nailed to the floor.

WINDOWS. When location permits, the windows of the dining room should reflect harmonies of light and color. There can be no more appropriate or enjoyable window decoration than that of

Collect all the lamps

stained or painted glass; the infinite variety in form and coloring offered in artistic and lovely designs makes an embarrassment of riches in this form of decoration. There are many pretty patented devices of semi-transparent imitations of stained glass that can be applied to ordinary glass windows when the expense of genuine stained or even painted glass can not be incurred.

WINDOW COVERINGS. The window draperies should temper but not exclude air and sunshine. When the outlook of dining-room windows is upon blank walls and paved yards, the unsightly prospect may be hidden, while permitting the free passage of light and air, by using Madras muslin curtains or any similar opaque drapery. Figured lace, cheese-cloth, or sheer nettings with dried fern or autumn leaves gummed upon them will serve this purpose.

CHINA. Select a stock pattern when buying china, preferably a standard design such as the well-known willow or onion design that can be readily replaced as pieces are broken. When possible, it is, of course, a good plan to have two sets of china, one for best, to be displayed in the china cabinet and only used upon special occasions, and another for ordinary wear, which may be less delicate and expensive.

DECORATIVE CHINA. When fine china or old pieces of plate are used in decorating the dining room, they should be disposed above the doors and fireplace on shelves or brackets.

It is true that if a given human being is, in general parlance, "sour, crusty, and crabbed," by placing about him the deftly executed designs of a true art, his nobler impulses are touched, his admiration excited, and almost unconsciously to himself, the three "ugly bears" vacate the ugly side of his character, a smile takes the place of a frown, a soft word the place of a harsh one—in fact, he is transformed into a pleasant being. This is not idle fancy but can be attested to by thousands of people.

—A. F. Fenstermaker, Decorator
Visitors Guide to Columbus, 1880

Sleeping Rooms

A rule to abide: where more than one person occupies a sleeping room, each individual should have a separate bed, even if the requirements of space or other conditions make it necessary for two or more beds to stand side by side.

BED SLIPS. Bed linen often falls short of covering the mattress completely while in use; hence, the extra slip is needed, especially to protect from dust the underside of the mattress. The slips can be removed and laundered twice a year or oftener when house-cleaning; the pillow covers may be removed oftener, if desired. Ticking treated in this way will be fresh and clean at the end of a dozen years' hard usage, when otherwise it would be so worn and soiled as to be unfit for use.

SHEETS. Linen is the best for comfort, appearance, and durability, but cotton sheeting is more commonly used, because it is less expensive. Buy unbleached linen or cotton, as it is not only less expensive, but much more durable and can be easily bleached when being laundered.

FEATHERS. The best feathers for beds and pillows are feathers plucked from live birds. Chicken, goose, or duck feathers may be preserved and used for beds or pillows by putting all the soft feathers together in a barrel as they are picked from the birds after scalding. Leave the barrel open to the sun and rain, covering it with an old screen to prevent the feathers from blowing about.

PROVIDE FOR VENTILATION. There is a superstition in many parts of the country that night air is injurious. In most localities this notion is groundless and misleading. If we do not breathe night air at night, pray what shall we breathe? Either it is necessary to breathe over and over the air that has been in the sleeping room all day or else to admit fresh air from outdoors; and whatever the danger in

Living out of doors

breathing night air, it is certainly less immediate than quick or slow suffocation from lack of ventilation.

SLEEP OUT OF DOORS IF POSSIBLE. Probably no practice would be more invigorating, healthful, or pleasurable than sleeping out of doors. In the vicinity of the great sanitariums, where sleeping out of doors has been proved to be a cure for consumption and other diseases, many persons have formed the habit of sleeping thus. Any porch somewhat excluded from view and in a sheltered location can be utilized. The porch should be screened and provided with storm curtains of tent canvas that can be drawn and buttoned like the curtains of a carriage. If the porch is used during the day a bunk or folding bed may be hinged to the wall on one side, with legs that will let down on the other. When folded up this may be concealed by a waterproof curtain. Or one of the so-called hammock beds may be suspended by hooks from the ceiling.

CHAPTER THREE

*A*PPOINTING YOUR KITCHEN

*There are very few housekeepers indeed who could not—by intelligent fore-
thought in planning and arranging the contents of the kitchen, pantry, and
storeroom—save themselves daily miles of useless traveling to and fro.*

Furniture

STOVE. First, the housekeeper must have a good stove or range, and
it is well for her to have the dealer at hand when it is put up, to see
that it draws well. A piece of hard, smooth asbestos board under the
range, cook stove, parlor stove, gas stove, or small oil stove is superior
to iron or zinc, because it is durable, easier to keep clean, and presents
a better appearance. The woodwork near stoves and the collars above
stovepipes, where they pass through the ceiling and side walls, may be
protected by the same material.

OVENS. Separate ovens, set apart, should be used for meat and pastry,
because the particles of fat which fly from the meat while it is baking
burn upon the sides of the oven and impart their odor and flavor to

delicate cakes and pastry. The bread and pastry ovens do not require to be so hot as those in which meat is baked, and means must be devised to moderate their heat when it is excessive. All the flues, and the top and bottom of the ovens, should be kept free from ashes, and the dampers should always be in good working order.

"WILSON L. GILL'S Stove and House Furnishing Store at No. 86 North High Street is the most complete and attractive store of this description in Columbus. The extensive selection of Base-Burners, Base Heaters, Parlor, Cook, Laundry and Tailor's stoves, Heating stoves for stores, offices, warerooms, warehouses and workshops, is a feature of this establishment. The stock of Tin Ware and Cooking Utensils is second to none in the city. The Table and Pocket Cutlery has been carefully selected, and the choice is very extensive. Remember the address, and do not fail to call."

—*Visitors Guide to Columbus,* 1880

SINK. The sink may be of iron or other metal, stone, or even wood lined with lead, tin, or zinc. But it should stand on four legs. The sink should be placed high enough so that the dishes may be washed without stooping. A small shelf or cupboard above the sink to contain soap, borax, washing powder, and various utensils will be found convenient.

To prevent pumps and water-pipes freezing in winter, take up the valve or sucker, and let all the water out of the trunk of pipe.

—A.S. Wright
Wright's Book of 3,000 Practical Receipts, 1869

Air is admitted to every part

SINK PIPES. All the waste pipes should be exposed to sun and air. Take away all woodwork from about the sink and paint the pipes and underpart the same color as the walls and woodwork. If the air is admitted freely to all parts, no moisture can accumulate to cause organic matter to decay, which produces diphtheria, typhoid, and other fevers. Physicians say that, when these diseases occur in any household, the first thing they look at is the sink and the arrangements for drainage about the kitchen door. Have the drainage carried into a covered cesspool a sufficient distance from the house, whence it will leach off into the soil; see that it does not leach into the well.

SINK-SIDE WORK TABLE. A bench or table, homemade if necessary, at the left of the kitchen sink and as large as the room will admit, is indispensable. Have the table overlap the edge of the sink and cover it with zinc, which will not rust. Turn up the zinc over a molding around the sides of the table, except at the end over the sink, so that water will drain back from it into the latter. Carry the zinc, if possible, eighteen inches or two feet up the kitchen wall behind the table and the sink. This is lasting, easily kept clean, and is not injured by hot pans or kettles. If scrubbed clean it can be used as a molding board; particles of dough which adhere to it can easily be scraped off with a knife.

TABLEWARE CABINET. Placing a china cabinet for the ordinary tableware just above the sink-side work table saves time and steps lost in walking from the sink to the table, and thence to pantry or closet.

STOOL. Provide a strong stool, high enough to allow sitting down at the sink to pare vegetables and for other purposes.

Kneading table

WORK TABLE. The kitchen table may be used as a work table if covered with oil cloth. This will last a long time if the table is padded with sheet wadding or several thicknesses of newspaper covered with an old sheet. Draw the padding smooth and tack it under the edge of the table.

KITCHEN CABINET. A good kitchen cabinet with metal bins for flour, meal, and other substances that mice are fond of is an investment which will save time and strength for the housekeeper and will be a money saver in the long run. These bins should be removable, so that they can be regularly washed, scalded, and dried.

Footstool. A footstool, convenient also as a receptacle for work, may be made of a common pine soap box; fasten the cover on the box with small hinges and put on the bottom four small casters. Line the box with plain white paper and cover. Excelsior, which can be got at any furniture store, is good to stuff the top and much cheaper than curled hair.

Bread-Warming Shelf. If you can have a three-cornered shelf of slate or sheetiron placed in a corner of the kitchen just above the bread block, it will be all the better, though a common wooden shelf, made very thin, will answer where you cannot get the other. A coal-oil lamp underneath will keep bread gently heated all night and will answer the double purpose of keeping a light burning, which most persons like to do at night and which they can do with scarcely any expense by using a coal-oil lamp.

Other Useful Objects to Have About

Washboard. Hang beside the sink a small washboard to rub out dishcloths and keep towels sweet and clean.

Dish Drain. Make a dish drain from an old dish pan by perforating the bottom with holes by means of a hammer and round wire nails. Place the draining pan to the left of the dish pan to avoid unnecessary handling. If the handles are front and back, as you face the dish pan, you will have fewer pieces of nicked china. If lye is used, and the dishwater is fairly hot and soapy, dishes rinsed with cold water will dry in the rack bright and shiny and not require wiping. Or, if thoroughly rinsed with hot water, they may be allowed to drain the same way.

Slate. A child's school slate hung on a nail, with a slate pencil attached by a strong cord, will be found a great convenience in ordering groceries. When any supplies run low, make a note on the slate of what is wanted; when the grocer calls, run over this list to refresh your mind. The slate is also useful for making a program each morning of the things to be done through the day. You will be surprised to find how quickly these things will be disposed of. When cooking or preparing company dinner, make a list of the articles to be prepared.

CONTAINERS. Stock the kitchen with:
- milk vessels of tin or earthenware, never stoneware;
- four buckets with close-fitting lids for setting aside milk for later—one for dinner, one for supper, one for breakfast, one for cooking purposes;
- bottles and jugs to hold yeast while rising and walnut catsup while sunning;
- stone jars to fill with brine in which to throw lemon peels to suit one's convenience and to store pickles, pack with shad, spices, and vinegar to set in boiling water for potted shad;
- demijohn or runlet for storing wine;
- glass jars for keeping preserves so they can be readily inspected;
- firkin to hold rolls of butter and to keep boiled pigs feet closely covered to prevent them from molding before they are fried;
- preserving kettle to put up corn in brine;
- small, common glasses for keeping jellies;
- wide-mouthed glass jars for keeping marmalade;
- piggin for taking up butter; and
- cotton bags to hang plum pudding for keeping.

TOPPERS. Keep a nice flat washed rock to weight down butter, beef, or tongues under brine; and stiff writing paper to dip in brandy and lay on top of preserves.

DINNER MATS. Dinner mats, either square or oval, made of two thicknesses of linen with an opening at one end to admit a square of asbestos, will prevent the hot tea or coffee pot or dishes containing hot food from injuring the tablecloth or the polished surface of the table.

STOVE MATS. Asbestos mats lined with wire have many uses about the stove. They may be placed in a hot oven to prevent cakes and pies from burning on the bottom and also on the top of the stove to prevent the contents of kettles and saucepans from burning. A small wire-lined asbestos mat, with a hole cut through the center but not through the wire, will be found useful for warming milk and other things in cups and small saucepans with rounded bottoms. The heat is applied to the bottom instead of the sides, and the vessel will not tip.

STOVE HOLDERS. At least a half dozen stove holders is not too many to have at hand in the kitchen at all times. Sew brass curtain rings, and hang on a nail near the stove, holders made of strong washable material, such as ticking or worn-out overalls, containing a removable square of asbestos. Or a large pair of loose mittens of canvas lined with asbestos may be fastened to a cord about two feet long and, when much cooking is to be done, slipped under the apron band so that both are suspended and always at hand. Some cooks say that two old wool stockings specially prepared and stitched together at the sides and ends, so as to admit of a removable square of asbestos between, make the best kitchen holders. Fold the legs inwardly three times to form a square, stitch across it, and also stitch it diagonally on the sewing machine in a crisscross pattern an inch or two apart to prevent wrinkling in the wash.

MATCH SAFE. Keep a stock of matches on a high, dry shelf in a covered earthen jar or tin box with a tight lid where they will be out of the way of children and safe from rats and mice. These animals are fond of phosphorus and will gnaw match heads if they can and often set them on fire. Have a covered match safe in each room where they are in frequent use; match safes fastened to sandpaper will be found a great convenience. To hold burnt matches, suspend a wineglass with a bit of ribbon from the gas jet.

ASH RECEPTACLE. Keep a sheet-iron pan or scuttle to take up ashes.

SLEEVE PROTECTORS. An old pair of stockings may be converted into useful sleeve protectors by cutting off the feet and hemming the cut edge. These may be drawn over the sleeves of a clean gown if necessary when washing dishes.

DISHCLOTHS. Save and use cloth flour sacks, sugar, salt, and cornmeal bags, which keep white and last longer than ordinary towel stuff. To wash flour sacks, turn them wrong side out and dust the flour from them and afterwards wash in cold water, since hot water will make a paste of the flour. You may also use scrim or cotton underwear crocheted about the edge or folded and hemmed double or the fiber of the so-called dishrag gourd, the seeds of which may be obtained from any seedman. Cheesecloth is good both for washing and wiping dishes, especially for drying silver and glassware. Best of all for many purposes is a small dish mop which permits of the use of boiling hot water and strong washing powder; with a little practice, the hands may be kept out of the water altogether.

Useful Tools and Utensils

USEFUL TOOLS FOR COOKING. Each kitchen must have a kitchen safe, a bread block in the corner furnished with a heavy iron beater, trays, sifters (with iron rims), steamers, colanders, a porcelain preserving kettle, perforated skimmers and spoons, ladles, long-handled iron forks and spoons, sharp knives and skewers, graters, egg beaters, plenty of extra bread pans, dippers and tins of every kind, iron molds for egg bread and muffins, wash pans, tea towels, bread towels and hand towels, plates, knives, forks and spoons for use of the servants, a pepper box, salt box and dredge box (filled), and last, but not least, a clock. As far as possible, use utensils made of iron, because they are stronger and cheaper than any other kind and, if perfectly clean, will grow better all the time. Let each article have its own place in the closet and kitchen, to which to restore it as soon as you have done using it.

USEFUL TOOLS FOR CLEANING. Convenient utensils are a swab made by fastening strips of linen or cotton to the end of a wooden handle; a soap shaker, which may be homemade; a pot scraper, which may be an ordinary clam shell; and a wire dish drainer, which may be hung on a neighboring wall. A line of strong cord or picture wire should be strung near at hand to hold the dishcloths and towels. A three-cornered wire drainer, fastened in the corner of the sink, will be found convenient to receive vegetable parings and also to strain the dishwater. A small shovel of cast iron, similar in shape to a fire shovel, will

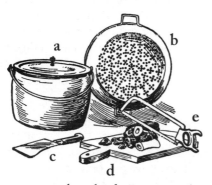

a. soup pot; b. colander; c. meat cleaver;
d. meat board with handle; e. meat saw

be a great convenience to lift scraps from the sink to the garbage can. Have one or more wood fiber brushes to clean dishes, kettles, and pans. The fibers are stiffer than bristles, and do more effective work. A whisk or two will clean an empty potato or gravy kettle as soon as the vessel is emptied.

LABOR-SAVING

TOOLS. I take it for granted that you are too intelligent to share in the vulgar prejudice against labor-saving machines. A raisin seeder costs a trifle in comparison with the time and patience required to stone the fruit in the old way. A good egg beater is a treasure. So with farina kettles, syllabub churns, apple corers, potato peelers, and slicers.

TOOLS FOR SLICING AND CORING. Vegetable cutters, made of tin and stored in a cylindrical case, come in several sizes appropriate for different tasks. The large tubes are used for cutting various garnishes and salad vegetables and for making little rounds of pastry and bread to be fried for garnishes; the medium sizes are useful for taking out the cores of fruit; and the smallest for cutting vegetables for soups.

TOOLS FOR STRAINING. Utensils for straining are a dripper, sifter, colander, and sieve. A potato masher is useful for beating materials through a colander, as is the purée sieve, made of perforated tin or very strong wire netting and set in a stout wooden frame. A very fine colander will serve for the purpose of making ordinary purées, especially the kind made with solid sides and a bottom of perforated tin. A hair sieve is recommended to strain pea-soup purée.

Tools for Pounding, Beating, and Rolling. The kitchen should have a mortar for pounding boiled tongue or ham to a smooth paste, for pounding truffles, for bruising walnuts for walnut catsup, and for beating Jordan almonds for almond cheese cake. A rolling pin or iron pestle is required to work and beat biscuit dough; and coarse towels are needed to enfold small reed birds to mash bones quite flat with a rolling pin.

Tools for Boiling. The bain-marie, or salt-water bath, is a deep iron or copper pan, partly filled with salted water, the temperature of which can be raised higher than that of fresh water and placed upon the back of the fire to contain saucepans whose contents require heating without boiling. This is one of the greatest of kitchen conveniences: Small saucepans or tin pails are set in the water bath to keep their contents hot after they are ready for the table. A card placed upon the handle of a saucepan indicates its contents without the trouble of removing the cover. A primitive bain-marie can be made with a dripping pan and several small tin pails or even empty tin cans. Soups, sauces, vegetables, and ragouts can be kept hot in this way without deteriorating. Other utensils necessary for boiling are a flat tin bucket to hold buttered sora, ortolans, and other small birds covered over a vessel of boiling water in order to keep the birds hot, juicy, and tender; a tin pail to hold tapioca cream in a kettle of boiling water to prevent the milk from scorching; a large tin cup to soft boil eggs; a fish kettle for boiling fish; a farina boiler for making soup; coarse cloth to tie up a bunch of parsley, thyme, and onion to throw into turtle soup when boiling, to sew up boned turkey to boil, and to sew around corned round of beef before boiling; needle and twine to sew up salmon in cloth to simmer for boiled salmon; and a net bag for boiling spices.

Tools for Steaming. The cook will need a clean broom to dip into salt water and pass over the mouths of oysters in the tub where they are being kept alive and fattened; coarse cloth to strain oyster liquor to rid it of all the scum and to dry washed oysters; and a steamer for holding washed shell oysters so juice will not escape from the shells when opened.

Bain-Marie

"Mr. Gill sells Flatider's Patent Domestic Steam Cooker, which is destined to bring about a complete revolution in culinary arrangements. Food is better cooked with much less labor, butcher's and coal bills are reduced, dyspepsia avoided, health promoted, and money saved, by the use of this article, which only has to be tried to be appreciated. One trial will convince the most skeptical of its value."

—*Visitors Guide to Columbus,* 1880

TOOLS FOR BROILING AND FRYING. Stock the kitchen with an oyster gridiron for broiling oysters over a quick fire and frying or broiling reed birds over a clear fire; a tin sheet for lifting boiled fish and for turning broiled fish; and a batter-cake turner for turning corn fritters and salmon steak when the side next to the fire is brown.

Tools for Preparing Dairy Products. The Dover Egg Beater is indispensable to housekeepers and deserves a word of special commendation. It froths eggs in less than a fourth of the time a spoon or an ordinary egg beater requires to froth them. Each kitchen should have two—one for the yolks and one for the whites. The cook will also desire a churn for making butter; a butter stick to wash and press butter; an old table cloth to wrap rolls of fresh butter; a butter print to print butter; the Krepp's Family Egg Tester to ascertain if an egg is sound; and a linen bag to drain cottage cheese.

Tools for Roasting Meats and Baking Vegetables. Surely nothing could be more worthy of a good word than the Economy Roaster, Baker, and Steamer. It consists of two sheet iron pans closely locked together, thus enabling any article of food cooked in them to retain flavor and nourishment better than by any other means of cooking. No attention is required after the pan enters your oven, as none of the steam arising from the meat is allowed to escape, it is absorbed back again and acts as a baster. Other devices to assist with roasting and baking are a lardering pin to introduce slips of clear fat bacon or salt pork into the surface of meat; a tin plate to place over veal steak to prevent hardness and drying as it cooks over coals and to place over sweet potatoes to prevent browning in a hot oven; a coarse cloth to wrap boned turkey for cooling after scalding and to tie up leg of mutton to cook; a needle and twine to sew up the cavities of partridges and pheasants filled with oysters; tape to tie beef before baking it in water and suet; sticks to place across the bottom of the dripping pan for roasting beef so it will not touch the water in the bottom; a piece of board (not pine) to tie shad on to roast before the fire; a small grating to lay in baking pan for basting baked fish; and stiff writing paper to put into partridges and to butter and pin over turkey, baked salmon, roast veal, and wild goose to keep them from becoming hard and dry while roasting.

Baking Tools. Baking requires a griddle for batter cakes; jelly-cake pans for making jelly cakes and white-mountain cakes; a straight side mold for baking fruit cake (as it turns out easier); a yellow dish for baking mush bread and a pudding dish for baking soft egg bread; a thick yellow earthenware dish, better than tin for baking puddings; a cake cutter for cutting out lemon jumbles after rolling; wafer irons for forming wafers; muffin rings to form Boston cream cakes; iron clads for baking sour-milk cakes; muslin for tying and boiling baked custard; cotton bags to boil plum pudding, sweetmeat pudding, and bread pudding; a blanket to wrap around dough in winter; a feather to dip in water and pass over dough to prevent crust from being too hard and to spread paste of rose water and egg whites on coffee cakes before baking; stiff writing paper to lay over baking bread to keep it from browning before heating through; and a closed cake-box to cover cake after cooling it and wrapping it in a thick napkin.

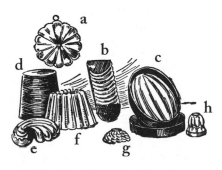

a. round fluted mold; b. French bread pan; c. melon mold; d. pudding mold; e. shell mold for jelly; f. deep fluted mold; g. individual shell mold for jelly or cream; h. individual jelly mold

Tools for Pickling. Pickling calls for a thorn or straw to puncture tomatoes for ripe tomato pickle; coarse cloths to squeeze chopped cabbage pickle until free from brine and to rub off walnuts for walnut pickle after they soak in fresh water; and brown paper to use, with a double piece of soft thick linen, to tie pickle jars tightly.

Tools for Making Preserves. Have porcelain or brass preserving kettles to heat fruits and sugar for marmalade and to make preserves and meat jelly (as for boned turkey); have a blanket to cover peach preserves as they sit in the sun until transparent and a flannel jelly bag for straining juice of boiled fruits.

The Storeroom

Groceries and supplies for a household of any size should, if possible, be bought in quantity and, therefore, every house should have a storeroom, appointed as follows.

MAKE A STOREROOM INEXPENSIVELY. A small storeroom can be made in a corner of the cellar at much less cost than is commonly supposed by putting up walls of concrete made of sand or gravel and cement. When furnished with a suitable door, this storeroom will be damp proof and free from dust, germs, and all other unsanitary pests. There should be a cellar window protected on the outside by wire netting and having on the inside a removable screen of cheese cloth to keep out the dust. If you would have wholesome food, keep the window down at the top, night and day, except in the coldest weather.

INCLUDE AMPLE SHELVING. Slat shelves painted with white paint and a coat of enamel may he built up in this storeroom back to back, with just enough room between them for a person to walk, in the same manner as book stacks in a library. Preserves, pickles, canned goods, butter, eggs, and other groceries can be stored year round in perfect safety.

HANG NETS FOR FRUIT. A suspended net or two should also be supplied for hanging lemons and oranges.

STOCK THE ROOM WITH EARTHENWARE. Earthenware jars are necessary for sugar, oatmeal, rice, tapioca, sago, barley, and spices. And, if it is wished to keep on hand the pound cake and fruit cake of our grandmothers (some cakes made from old-fashioned recipes given in this book will keep for years), no snugger quarters for their preservation can be found than earthen jars with tight-fitting lids inside the dry storeroom.

KEEP AN ACCOUNT BOOK. This is the room where you should enter the date when each store is bought and the price paid for it in your account book.

MAKE AN OUTDOOR CUPBOARD. Have you an outdoor cupboard in which to keep milk, meat, and fish during the cool weather of early spring and fall? A dry-goods box with a hinged locked door, nailed above the reach of cats and dogs against the arbor that covers the kitchen door, will save many a journey to the storeroom. It should have holes bored in the ends to allow a current to circulate through it, for food will keep fresher and sweeter in the open air.

Recommendation for Shopping

Groceries, vegetables and wooden ware
Can be bought for money everywhere,
But lowest for cash and best, you will see
At Mahache, Muchlenbruch & Company
18 South Main Street, Marysville, Ohio

—An advertisement in the
Centennial Buckeye Cook Book, 1876

The Kitchen Garden

I wish all my fair sisters would set apart a portion of their home grounds for the garden. A good flower garden exerts a powerful influence upon the aesthetic side of the home life, and the vegetable garden contributes to the family's health and economy. An area of land cultivated as a kitchen garden will easily supply the family table with one hundred dollars worth of vegetables every year.

Best for the lady who tends the garden is that life-giving something in the very smell of the ground, especially in the soft springtime. And when the long summer days are come, when the lady drops her endless sewing and gathers what she has grown in anticipation of preparing a fresh meal—a vase of colorful blooms upon the table to meet the family when they sit—she will come back with lighter step and rosy cheeks. This is not romance, but sound common sense.

START SMALL. Most women have their time quite fully occupied with the supervision of household matters. They would like to have some flowers, because a certain amount of work among them is refreshing, really a resting spell because of its change from the monotony of work indoors. The cultivation of a small garden will not involve more labor than they can perform in odd spells; but if they attempt too much, the flowers, if they would grow them well, will call for so much attention from them that the idea of rest and recreation is destroyed and they will fail to enjoy them. Begin cautiously and enlarge the field of operation as you feel justified in doing so.

PREPARE SOIL CAREFULLY. To prepare the earth for seeds or small plants or for filling pots or window boxes, mix one part by bulk of well rotted manure, two parts of good garden loam, and one part of sharp fine sand. Choose for this purpose manure which has been thoroughly rotted but not exposed to leaching from the weather. Mix all together in a heap, stir well with the shovel, sift and place in bores or in the bed prepared for the seed. If convenient, bake the soil for an hour in a hot oven. This will kill all weed seed and spores of fungus disease.

Uprooting sapling with horse and chain

To Make a Rustic Flower Stand. Take a stump up by the roots, turn it upside down, put it firmly in the ground and sow flower seeds in it. The rustic sticks used by nurserymen for hanging baskets, urns, etc., are the knotted roots of the bush known as greenbrier, common in the woods in northern Ohio.

Protect Plants from the Weather. To protect small plants from heat drive stakes into the ground slanting toward the north and lean boards against them so as to shade the rows. Or use light frames on lath or wooden slate and cover them with cotton cloth. To protect crops planted in winter from cold and give an early start in the spring, set the stakes slanting to the south and lean boards against them on the north side. Or cover with a mulch of manure, straw or leaves. But take care that this is not so thick as to keep the air from the plants and also see that it is free from injurious weeds. To start early plants in the northern half of the United States build a hot bed. This is simply a box sunk in the ground and heated from below by means of a bed of stable manure or otherwise. It contains a layer of soil for the seed bed and is protected by a cover of window sash filled with glass. Hot beds may be temporary or permanent.

Choose Old Seed Dealers. If you send to the florist for seed—and it is always advisable to do that, for he makes a specialty of seed growing and knows how to produce the best—be sure to patronize a reliable dealer. There are always men in all kinds of business who are not to be trusted. The old seed farms are all reliable, I think; the fact of their continuance in business proves that, for if they were not they would, after a little, lose customers and give up.

Form a Seed Club. The packages of seeds put up by most seed growers generally contain more than one person will care to use. It is good to club together in a country neighborhood. The cost will be less, and there will be seeds enough to divide among half a dozen persons.

Gardening Advice from Ohioans

HOW TO RAISE INDIAN CORN. Plow as early in the spring as the season will permit with three horses abreast, seven or eight inches deep; harrow and roll until the ground is thoroughly pulverized; plant from the first to the fifteenth of May, with Dickey drill, three or four inches deep in rows three and one-half feet apart. As soon as the corn begins coming up, harrow again with a light harrow thoroughly, giving no attention to rows. When the plants are about three or four inches high, plow with a walking or double-shovel plow, with shovels about two inches wide, close to the corn—the closer the better—and quite deep. For the rest of the culture use common-sized shovels and plow about every eight days until the corn is about three and a half or four feet high.

—Mr. C. Phellis, Sr.

THE RASPBERRY. Flourishes in almost any soil and will thrive in neglected fence corners, but a good loam, well cultivated, gives the best results. It bears liberal manure and should be planted in fall or early spring, three feet apart in rows from six to nine feet wide, or for garden planting much closer. Summer pruning is now practiced by all good cultivators, which consists in pinching or cutting off the shoots as soon as they are two feet high, which causes them to branch out with strong laterals; these are cut back according to their strength in the winter. In autumn or winter the old cones and the weak new ones should be cut away and only the strong and healthy left for the next crop. Trained thus no support is needed. Leaf and woods mold, crushed sugar cane stalks, straw, grass, chips, ashes, and rotted tanbark are all good mulching material, and placed close around the roots insure big crops.

—J. S. Robinson

Sure Slot for Rose Slugs. About the first of June, small worms make their appearance on the rose bushes, and in a very few days eat every leaf on them. To destroy these pests, take four gallons water, add one tablespoon paris green, stir thoroughly, and apply to the bushes with a garden syringe or watering pot, early in the morning; keep the water well stirred or shaken while applying, or the last in the pot will be too strong and kill the leaves of the bushes.

—Mr. C. Phellis, Sr.

Remedy for the Plum Curculio. Prepare a muslin spread large enough to cover the ground under the tree as far out as the branches extend; give the tree a vigorous shake or two, and the insects will drop off upon the sheet, and may be readily gathered up and dispatched. In the few first hot days of spring the insect begins its work of destruction in earnest and the process of shaking should then begin and be carried on vigorously morning, noon and evening, and kept up as long as any curculios are found, seldom over a period of twenty-five days, unless the season is cool and backward. Of course there will be a stray insect now and then till the plum changes color for ripening, but the damage will be slight. The writer has tried many remedies but all have failed miserably except this, which has repeatedly saved his crop of plums when all other trees in the neighborhood have failed.

—J. H. Shearer

Protecting Cabbage from Worms. Mix wheat bran and buckwheat flour together and sprinkle dry over cabbage. It does not matter about quantity.

—Miss Abbie Phellis Baker
The Centennial Buckeye
Cook Book, 1876

PART THREE

Nurturing Yourself and Your Family

CHAPTER ONE

ℰNCOURAGING HEALTHY PERSONAL HABITS

Health is the foundation of all beauty; there can be no solid and enduring loveliness without health.

Preserving Vitality

ℰvery person is born with a certain stock of vitality, which cannot be increased, but which may be husbanded or expended rapidly. Within certain limits each person has a choice, to live fast or slow, to live abstemiously or intensely, to draw the little amount of life over a large space, or condense it into a narrow one.

TAKE CARE TO INCREASE LONGEVITY. The person who lives abstemiously, who avoids all stimulants, takes light exercise, never overtasks himself, indulges no exhausting passions, feeds his mind and heart on no exciting material, lets nothing ruffle his temper, and keeps his "accounts with God and man squared up" is sure, barring accidents, to spin out life to the longest limit which it is possible to attain.

I am fifty-one years old today. Gray hairs are getting into my brow; hair grows perceptibly thinner, but no baldness yet. I read without glasses but my eyes inflame if I read or write many hours by lamplight; more fleshy and full-stomached, with shorter breath; a few twinges of rheumatism; a fondness for a nap after dinner; teeth pretty good, but several plugged and a few gone; whiskers rapidly whitening. These are the symptoms of old age. On the other hand, a youthful and elastic spirit: fondness for all young people and their employments and amusements. A fresh, ruddy complexion and considerable physical strength and activity almost persuade me that I am still in my youth.

—Rutherford B. Hayes
Journal entry on October 4, 1873

KNOW HOW NOT TO HASTEN DEATH. The person who lives intensely, who feeds on high-seasoned food, whether material or mental, fatigues the body or brain by hard labor, exposes himself to inflammatory disease, seeks continual excitement, gives loose rein to passion, frets at every trouble, and enjoys little repose is burning the candle at both ends and is sure to shorten his days.

EXPEL YOUR EMOTIONS, NO MATTER YOUR SEX. Probably most persons have experienced the effect of tears in relieving great sorrow. It is even curious how feelings are allayed by free indulgence in groans and sighs. A French physician contends that groaning and crying are two grand operations by which nature allays anguish; that those patients who give way to their natural feelings more speedily recover from accidents and operations than those who suppose it unworthy a person to betray such symptoms of cowardice as either to groan or cry.

BE HAPPY NOW. This looking forward to enjoyment does not pay. From what I know, I would as soon chase butterflies for a living or bottle moonshine for cloudy nights. The only true way to be happy is to take the drops of happiness as God gives them to us every day.

Working

DO YOUR WORK SLOWLY. When wives work at something they become so interested in it they find themselves in an utterly exhausted condition; their ambition to complete a thing, to do some work well, sustains them till it is completed. Work by the day, if you must work at all, and not by the job. It is more economical in the end to see how little work you can do in an hour, instead of how much. It is slow, steady, continuous labor which brings health and strength, and a good digestion. Fitful labor is ruinous.

TAKE YOUR RESPITES. It is a duty to work and to be industrious; and it is also a duty to be temperate in your work. It is refreshing and strengthening to drop the oar occasionally and drift with the tide; you may not accomplish so much within a given time, but the voyage of your life will be longer for a little respite.

We sleep, but the loom of life never stops, and the pattern which was weaving when the sun went down is weaving when it comes up in the morning.

—Henry Ward Beecher (1813–1887)
President, Ohio's Lane Theological Seminary

BALANCE YOUR TIME. Have certain hours to work and work with a will; have certain hours to read and think of nothing else; have certain hours to spend with your family in social talk, which may be made instructive as well as interesting and from which both you and they may receive lasting benefit.

BREATHE AND MOVE. The best medicines for all of us are air and activity. When, after long sitting, the circulation becomes torpid and the brain weary, set your window open for a few moments, even in midwinter. And if a short brisk walk outdoors during the interval be impracticable, go through a series of gymnastics or wrestle with imaginary burglars, and you will not find your minutes thrown away.

There is not enough exercise in this way of life. I try to make up by active gymnastics before I dress when I get up, by walking rapidly in the lower hall and the greenhouse after each meal for perhaps five to ten minutes, and a good hand rubbing before going to bed.

—Rutherford B. Hayes
White House Diary, March 18, 1878

Eating

It is most important to health that meals should be taken at suitable times and that ample use of the teeth should be made before swallowing.

SATISFY EMPTINESS EARLY. Persons who rise early and cannot conveniently obtain their full morning meal for two or three hours would do well to secure the provision of some slight refreshment of a light and simple kind, to be taken before they address themselves to the first duties of the day.

PREPARE ABUNDANT BREAKFASTS. This meal is second only in importance to the dinner, especially when any extreme mental labor is demanded of the members of the family. Our national habits demand that the breakfast shall be hot and abundant and that there shall be such successive variety that the appetite shall always be stimulated.

TAKE TIME WITH THE MID-DAY MEAL. The natural time for dinner would appear to vary with the habits of life between the hours of noon and three o' clock. Plenty of time should be given to this meal, the food taken slowly in small morsels. And, if practicable, a considerable period of rest for body and mind should be secured between dining and returning to the ordinary duties and labors of the day.

TAKE THE EVENING MEAL EARLY. There should not be long intervals between the meals, nor should the principal meal be taken late in the day. The digestive organs partake of the weariness and reduction of power which the rest of the body experiences after the lapse of many hours of wakefulness and activity and, if then required to exercise their functions upon abundance of solid food, cannot perform their work satisfactorily.

BE OF CALM MIND WHILE EATING. Not only regularity of mealtimes, but comfort and good order at meals, will conduce in a great degree the due and satisfactory enjoyment, and hence good digestion, of food. It is a well-known fact that fear, anger, vexation, and anxiety felt at the time of eating prevent the proper decoction of food by the stomach; and so, to a certain extent, must all other perturbations of the mind.

ATTEND TO YOUR APPEARANCE FOR THE TABLE. Napery, spotless as newly fallen snow, dishes of graceful form and well arranged, around which cluster smiling faces—these make a dinner of herbs a place where happy hearts hold high festival. The mother may have had to cook the meal herself, helped by her daughter, but she puts on a fresh collar or bit of lace before coming to the table. The father brushes his mind as well as his coat, while the elder children see that the younger ones are presentable; and then the meal begins, slowly, as an entertainment in which fine courtesy is the rule and never the exception.

USE COMPANY MANNERS EVERY DAY. If your children never see bright silver unless there is company, you cannot wonder at their making looking glasses of the bowls and the spoons and handling the forks awkwardly. Press upon them early that what is nice enough for Papa is nice enough for the President; I have noticed that where there is a wide difference between family and company table furniture, there usually exists a corresponding disparity between everyday and company manners. Let courtesies more than courtly be daily cultivated.

Purifying the Blood

Sherley Dare, in answering correspondents through the *Toledo Blade Household* says: "The safest and quickest prescription for clearing the blood is to eat a raw onion, finely minced, at breakfast; the whole of a common sized onion is enough, and a dose of charcoal or ground coffee, and brushing the teeth, will deodorize the breath. The onion can be taken with salt and vinegar as a salad. Consumptives find this of benefit."

—Dr. Chase's Third Last and Complete
Receipt Book and Household Physician, 1903

Bathing

A daily bath for the whole body is not too much. Health may not absolutely require this, but there are few persons who would not be benefited by a complete washing of the skin from head to foot, at least once every day. The feet need washing as much as the head, as perspiration upon them is very abundant. Feet that are cased in wool and leather are not excepted from this necessity of cleansing. Digestion is freer when water is applied above the organs of digestion; and the washing of the chest helps one to breathe more freely. Bathing makes the limbs supple, and it opens the muscles to breathe from, if such an unscientific statement may be permitted. All will agree that in the second month of summer a daily bath is a luxury not to be omitted, but in winter it is hardly less necessary, and the reaction which follows makes it a luxury even in the most inclement season.

—*Peterson's Magazine,* June 1872

SET A WEEKLY BATH. A set time for each member of the family to take the weekly bath will tend to promote the convenience of the household. Saturday night and Sunday morning are probably the best times for most persons. The weekly bath thus becomes a preparation for Sunday-morning toilet, which is ordinarily the most careful and elaborate of the week. The bath should be from 80 to 95 degrees Fahrenheit.

TAKE A DAILY HAND BATH. In addition to the ordinary weekly bath, there should also be added the daily morning sponge or hand bath. Simply dip a small quantity of water from the bowl or basin and wet the entire body—not omitting the eyes, face, neck, and feet—and then follow such ablutions, first, with a thorough dry-towel rubbing and, next, with a vigorous bare-hands or coarse-towel rubbing. Those who are less robust may obtain some of the benefits of the sponge bath by substituting a vigorous rubbing with a towel or flesh brush each morning.

USE COLD WATER. If begun in summer, there is no danger of contracting a cold from the bath, and as the weather gradually grows colder in the fall, no shock will come to the already acclimated system. Then, even though the sleeping room should be so cold that ice would form in the pitcher during the night, the morning bath will be taken without a shudder, and the invigoration and healthy glow which will follow will be more than a recompense and reward for the resolution, time, and effort it costs.

ABIDE THESE RULES FOR BATHING:

- Do follow the daily bath with a bath of sun and air; follow the weekly hot-water bath with a change of clothing.
- Do wet the head first in all baths.
- Don't bathe early in the morning on an empty stomach unless you are vigorous and strong enough to stand it. The best time for you may be two or three hours after breakfast.
- Don't take any kind of a bath within two hours after eating a hearty meal.
- Do wash the body with water to which has been added two tablespoons of ammonia—the compound spirits. It is perfectly harmless and will fortify against the odor of perspiration.
- Do stand a minute in the cold air after removing the clothing and before applying the water, when bathing in winter. This will lessen the shock from cold water.
- Don't stay too long in the water; get out before you begin to feel chilly.

Care of Teeth and Breath

CLEAN THE TEETH DAILY. The teeth should be thoroughly washed with a soft brush and warm water at least once a day, and that before retiring. Cleanliness will preserve and beautify any teeth, unless they are actually diseased. All pastes and toothwashes should be discarded. Do not use the highly advertised preparations, however delightful they are. Chalk and myrrh are excellent and safe dentifrices, as is castile soap. After using the tooth brush, rinse it in clean cold water and dry it ready for further use.

The following is a simple and cheap preparation [for tooth powder], and is pretty good. Take of prepared chalk and fine old Windsor soap pulverized well, in proportion of about six parts of the former to one of the latter. Soap is a very beneficial ingredient of tooth powder.

—H. W. Morey, D.D.S.
The Centennial Buckeye Cook Book, 1876

SEEK CARE WHEN NEEDED. When tartar accumulates upon the teeth, it can only be removed by a dentist. For diseased teeth, resort should be had to a good dentist at once. Delay is fatal, for the diseased tooth decays rapidly and will have a like effect on those that are sound. Sometimes the teeth become sore and there is a brown coating about the sockets. If this is not attended to, the teeth become loose, protrude, and finally drop out.

EMPLOY THE BEST DENTISTS. Teeth, like the eyes, should only be treated by the most experienced and reliable of practitioners.

Care of the Skin

A clear, polished skin can only be had by observing three things— temperance, cleanliness, and exercise.

RESTORE YOUR BRIGHTNESS. Exercise in the open air, plain food, early rising, and a bath once or twice a week will prove the best beautifiers for the complexion and will change a skin as rough as a nutmeg grater to one as smooth and brilliant as satin, restoring that youthful brightness that so many ladies have lost.

WATCH YOUR DIET. The inordinate use of liquors or strong coffee, greasy food, or hot biscuits will tell upon the finest complexion in time. The young lady who devours pickles, sits up half the night reading novels, and lounges round the house the next day can never expect that clear, fresh, peach-like complexion which she longs for so ardently.

ADD BRAN TO THE BATH. Freshness of the skin is prolonged by a simple secret: the tepid bath in which bran is stirred, followed by long friction till the flesh fairly shines. A bran bath should be taken at least once a week. Place the bran in little thin muslin bags and drop in the bathtub to soak about two hours before using.

BATHE WITH RAIN WATER. Rain water is the best by far to use for the toilet. Little or no soap is needed with it, as it is very soft and easily removes all dirt. In a city house, the best way to obtain rain water is to keep a tub on the roof or in the yard to catch it.

BE CAREFUL TO:
* Dry with a fine soft cloth, always rubbing downward. Be sure to dry the face thoroughly. Quick and brisk rubbing is not good for the face.
* Use soap very sparingly on the face and hands and only pure white Castile soap then. Although it is not so agreeable to use as others, it is perfectly safe and pure.

AVOID COSMETICS. Ladies cannot be too cautious about using cosmetics, however loudly they may be advertised or however highly they may be recommended. One of the most famous beauties of the last century, not content with her natural beauty, sought to enhance it and used cosmetics, which caused her death. Physicians are continually called on to treat ladies suffering from the use of injurious cosmetics.

KNOW THE CAUSES OF POOR SKIN. There is some good reason why a woman has a coarse or mottled skin. Either the digestion is bad, the blood impure, or she does not bathe sufficiently. If the face is washed often and the rest of the body only occasionally, all the impurities which are in the skin must come out through the pores of the skin on the face. Thus, wash the body at least once a day. Powdered oatmeal rubbed on the skin after bathing also proves beneficial. Neither should you sit too near or too long before an open fire. The heat will harm the smooth texture of the skin, as would harsh or cold air.

A Plan to Improve the Complexion

An inquiry through the *Toledo Blade* for a plan to improve the complexion by removing pimples, etc., was made in the following words: "My complexion is sallow and bad, my skin pimply all over. I am run down and want to feel alive again. What is the matter, and what is to be done?" To this inquiry the editor of the "Household Department" made such a common-sense reply that I give it a place, hoping that every one needing such an alternative effect will adopt her suggestions and save the necessity of taking something which is more of a medicinal character. She says:

"The matter is that the blood is thoroughly vitiated and improving it must be a matter of time. Spring diet should do the work of medicine, largely. And first in importance are salads of all sorts . . . from the pepper-grass and the watercress to the tender turnip, mustard, and cabbage . . . all good to mix for some of the most inviting salads.

But the vegetable which is most beneficial and ranks as a medicine and purifier of the finest sort, is one, though its stigma is now removed in polite society, is under the ban in ordinary circles. The virtues of the onion render it a pharmacopoeia in itself. Eaten raw, with or without vinegar, it is the most effective purifier of the blood known. As a toilet prescription, it will do as much to refine the complexion, renew the hair, and remove spots as any article known. Do not hesitate to eat onions freely, since the use of a toothbrush and a dose of charcoal will remove the odor. To get their full benefit, eat raw onions and their young shoots at breakfast, as a salad, with bread and butter.

> —*Dr. Chase's Third Last and Complete*
> *Receipt Book and Household Physician,* 1903

Care of Hands and Arms

A beautiful hand is a poem in itself, and many are the devices resorted to, to keep it white and shapely.

ALWAYS WEAR GLOVES WHEN:

- *Housekeeping.*
- *Outdoors.*
- *Sleeping.* Sleeping in soft, white kid gloves, after rubbing mutton tallow on the hands, will keep them soft and white. Large mittens worn at night filled with wet bran or oatmeal keep the hands white, in spite of the disfiguring effects of housework.

KEEP NAILS CLEAN AND TRIMMED. Nothing is more disgusting than a finger with a black border at the end. A well-kept nail will be smooth, shiny, and rosy. Filbert-shaped nails are esteemed the handsomest. Trim them with rounded corners.

Care of the Feet

It is astonishing how much perfect cleanliness and care will do for the appearance of the feet and even the size. It is true, as a few months' trial will abundantly demonstrate.

SOAK FEET INTERMITTENTLY. One way to keep the feet in a healthy state is to soak them several times a week in hot water into which a handful of salt has been thrown.

SOAK FEET NIGHTLY. Another excellent treatment is to soak them at night for 15 minutes in hot soap suds. Then rub them well and with a ball of pumice stone rub off all the superfluous skin, after which olive oil or oil of sweet almonds may be rubbed in.

WEAR PROPER SHOES. India rubbers should be worn only in rainy, muddy weather. They prevent the circulation of air and cause a perspiration that is offensive. Insoles are better for the feet than rubbers. Thick-soled leather shoes are better for every-day use. A shoe too short will deform any foot in time.

Care of the Hair

The most bewitching face unshaded by soft, shiny hair, and a goodly share of it, cannot lay claim to beauty.

BRUSH FREQUENTLY. Hair requires continual brushing. Each morning, when hair is most pliable, it should receive a thorough brushing lasting at least ten minutes. The most dry and harsh hair will yield to this treatment and become soft, glossy, and strong.

USE SOFT BRUSHES. The brush used should be soft and clean. It is a bad practice to use a very hard brush under the impression that it stimulates the scalp. It may do that, but at the expense of the hair, which it breaks and snarls. Brushes should be washed in tepid water to which a little ammonia is added, care being taken not to wet the back of the brush. The bristles should be rinsed thoroughly and dried in the open air.

WASH WITHOUT SHAMPOO. The head should be washed at least once a week, but shampooing is a great detriment to the beauty of the hair. Soap fades the hair, often turning it a yellow. Brushing is the only safe method of removing the dust from the head, with the occasional use of the whites of eggs.

AVOID HAIR DYE. We have known of cases of paralysis of the brain occasioned by the use of hair dyes which their makers asserted were "perfectly harmless." Most of the hair dyes have a base of lead, caustic alkalies, limes, litharge, and arsenic, all of which burn the hair.

AVOID POMADES AND OIL. The use of oils and pomades is never desirable. Animal fats are more injurious than vegetable oils, as they heat the cuticle and become rancid, acting eventually as a depilatory. If you find a split or forked hair, clip off the extreme end to promote growth.

Care of the Eyes

The eyes, "those windows of the soul," are terribly abused. Late hours, reading by bad lights, straining them by overuse are all destructive to the eyes' beauty.

TURN UP THE LIGHTS. A darkened room is not the best; indeed, it will weaken the eyes. A good steady, strong light is more favorable.

REMOVE STYS WITH TEA. These painful little affections are easily removed by placing a little tea in a bag. Pour on boiling water to moisten it and apply to the eye warm. Keep it on all night. A second application will perhaps be necessary.

EYE WASH. Mix and bottle two grains sulphate of zinc, one-half grain sulphate of morphine, and one ounce distilled water. Drop in the eye (a drop or two at once), then wink the eye several times so that the wash may reach all the parts. Keep quiet and do not use the eyes for about an hour. This wash is for bloodshot eyes, and when used it will produce quite a smarting sensation.

Recreation

Play makes you wish to work; work makes you wish to play.

LADIES, GO OUT. A woman is not a hot-house plant, to be kept indoors under a glass case. She flourishes best when she opens the door and walks abroad, courts the free air and the blessed light of heaven. If this simple philosophy of health were better understood, and such outdoor occupation and exercise were to become a universal habit, we should soon have a new race of American women.

WALK ACTIVELY, FOR EXERCISE. It is better for a person in health and of sedentary habits to walk in the rain rather than not walk at all. The exercise should be active and not consist of either strolling or sauntering out of doors or even amateur gardening. People will be often heard to say that they have plenty of exercise about the house. What is wanted for the health is exercise without fatigue; for fatigue is exhaustion.

MAKE FUN AT HOME. Gayety is one of the surest symptoms of moral health; it is indispensable in childhood, and I doubt whether it can be dispensed with in after life. Don't be afraid of a little fun at home. Half an hour of merriment round the lamp and firelight of a home blots out the remembrance of many a care and annoyance during the day, and the best safeguard that your children take with them into the world is the unseen influences of a bright little domestic sanctum. Boys and girls are blessedly guarded when they find all their faculties exercised at home. They do not care to roam, and so they are detained from a thousand outside dangers.

The Benefits of Reading

The "sweet society of books" is a never-failing source of entertainment, comfort, and consolation. Books and periodicals should be angels to every household. They are urns to bring us the golden fruits of thought and experience from other minds and other lands.

READ ONLY THE BEST BOOKS. The books which start a young person aright, which impart the right principles, inspire with high and holy ambition. A critical reading of history and biography widens the view, ripens the judgment, and enables the intellect to better understand the issues of life and grapple with its problems. In science, begin with the simple and intelligible books, and, if you desire, let the more abstruse follow later.

These words dropped into my childish mind as if you should accidentally drop a ring into a deep well. I did not think of them much at the time, but there came a day in my life when the ring was fished up out of the well, good as new.

—Harriet Beecher Stowe (1811–1896)
Active in Ohio's Underground Railroad and
author of *Uncle Tom's Cabin*

READ WITH ABSORPTION. In reading, as in other things, give yourself absorbingly to what you are at. Read only as much as you can read thoroughly; more than that is never helpful, but is often hurtful. Take up a single subject and study it carefully. You cannot read everything, and do not be so unwise as to attempt it.

READ NEWSPAPERS SELECTIVELY. Get the best daily and read only sparingly; to keep informed on current events, read a reliable weekly. Spend no time upon the ordinary daily newspaper. The prevalent desire to know the news of the very latest minute leads editors to publish rumors, to write accounts of events before they take place, and to tell of sensational things that never happen at all.

READING ALOUD. No home exercise could be more appropriate and pleasing than for one member to read aloud for the benefit of all. As the fruits of the trees of the earth's soil are most enjoyed around the family board, so should those that mature upon mental and moral boughs be gathered around by the entire household. Read to your children and encourage them to read to you.

CHAPTER TWO

REARING CHILDREN

On Friday, the 4th, at 2 p.m., Lucy gave birth to our first child—a son. I hoped, and had a presentiment almost, that the little one would be a boy. How I love Lucy, the mother of my boy! Sweetheart and wife, she had been before, loved tenderly and strongly as such, but the new feeling is more 'home-felt,' quiet, substantial, and satisfying. For the 'lad' my feeling has yet to grow a great deal. I prize him and rejoiced to have him, and when I take him in my arms begin to feel a father's love and interest, hope and pride, enough to know what the feeling will be if not what it is. I think what is to be his future, his life. How strange a mystery all this is! This to me is the beginning of a new life. A happy one, I believe.

—Rutherford B. Hayes
Diary entry, Cincinnati,
November 6, 1853

Dietary Guidelines for Little Ones

The quality of food intended for little children should be carefully studied, as the firmness of their flesh and the hardness of their bones is so dependent upon it.

GENERAL GUIDELINES FOR ALL CHILDREN. Let nutrition, variety, and the time of year guide your selections. Every care must be taken to supply children with a variety and abundance of nutritious and digestible food, in which fruit, the cereals, vegetables, milk, mutton, beef, and poultry should be included together with simple sweets and plain puddings chiefly composed of milk, eggs, and flour or bread.

PARENTS, MONITOR THEIR INTAKE. Every abnormal appetite should be modified by judicious control on the part of the parents or nurse if the child is to receive the care its helpless condition imposes upon its natural protectors. When children show any marked preference for special foods, care should be taken to modify their tastes.

LIMIT THEM TO WATER AND MILK. Tea, coffee, and stimulants should be avoided and plenty of cool fresh water used as the habitual drink. And don't forget milk: wherever milk is used plentifully, there the children grow into robust men and women; wherever the place is usurped by tea, we have degeneracy swift and certain.

SERVE EACH MEAL THUS. The breakfast should be early and plentiful. Mid-day dinners should be varied and always hot; indeed, all food is most digestible when warm, and composed of some plain meat dish, at least two vegetables, and a simple pudding. Soup is invaluable for children, but it must be plain. The supper, given about two hours before retiring, should be light and nutritious and may include warm bread and milk, any form of porridge and milk, custard, bread and butter, simple stewed fruits, and either cool water or cocoa as a beverage.

Dietary Suggestions for Children under Three

LIMIT HIS FARE. Confine a child under three years of age to a very limited bill of fare. Grant him novel food sparingly and with discretion as to kind. His stomach is too delicate an organ to be tampered with. Let milk—scalded or boiled, as a rule—be the staple, mixed with farina, barley, or something of the sort. Let him munch Graham bread and light crackers freely. Remove far from him hot bread and griddle cakes.

Save the babies

COOK ALL FOOD THOROUGHLY. The numerous varieties of farinaceous substances, such as biscotine, farina, rice-flour, and arrowroot, however nourishing may be their properties when rightly prepared, are harsh and drastic when underdone.

SUPPLY PLENTY OF BREAD. Homemade bread should be eaten in preference to the baker's bread, because in baker's bread some of those valuable nutritive parts are destroyed, and while it satisfies hunger, it does not nourish the body.

LET THE GROWTH OF HIS TEETH GUIDE YOU. Nature's supply is seldom in advance of the demand. If he did not need what the teeth are designed to chew, you may be sure they would not be given him. The cutting of the eighth incisors or front teeth, which occurs usually during the twelfth month, may be taken as nature's indication that the child requires other food than milk. Rare beef and well-boiled mutton, tender roast, or boiled chicken and turkey are safe. Withhold fried meats of every description. Do not let him touch veal or pork in any shape. Mince the meat very finely to save his digestive apparatus all unnecessary work.

GIVE TO HIM THESE FOODS. Mealy old potatoes—never new or waxy—and young onions, boiled in two waters; fresh asparagus, green peas, and dry sweet potatoes should suffice for vegetables, with, of course, rice and hominy. For dessert, once in a while, a simple custard, a taste of homemade ice cream, rice and farina puddings, Graham hasty pudding, and the inner part of a well-roasted apple.

DO NOT GIVE HIM THESE. Hundreds of infants have been killed by the mistakes of parents in giving them improper foods. Never feed the baby at the table from the food prepared for other members of the family; the table foods may be poisonous to the infant. The skin of an apple is as bad for him as a bit of your kid gloves would be, and that of a grape more indigestible than sole leather. Raisins are unfit for anybody to eat. Pulp and pits, they are poisonous for baby. Never give a child under two years of age ham, bacon, or pork in any form; cabbage, pickles, or other succulent vegetables; coffee, tea, beer, wine, cider or any other alcoholic liquor of any kind; bananas, berries, or other fruit except prune juice and stewed or baked apple. Ditto, pickles, pastry, and preserves.

Recipes for the Nursery

Some of the finest children I have ever seen were reared upon this diet.

CONDENSED MILK. This is perhaps the safest substitute for the "good milk from one cow," which few mothers in town can procure. Keep the can in a cool place and mix according to directions.

FARINA. Stir one large tablespoon Hecker's Farina, wet up with cold water, into one cup boiling water (slightly salted) in the farina kettle (i.e, one boiler set within another, the latter filled with hot water). Boil 15 minutes, stirring constantly until it is well thickened. Then add one cup fresh milk, stirring it in gradually, and boil 15 minutes longer. Sweeten with two teaspoons white sugar and give to the child as soon as it is cool enough. You may make enough in the morning to last all day; warming it up with a little hot milk as you want it. Keep in a cold place. Do not get it too sweet and cook it well.

ARROWROOT. Stir arrowroot paste of two teaspoons best Bermuda arrowroot wet with cold water into one cup boiling water with one small pinch of salt; stir and boil five minutes or until it is clear; add two even teaspoons white sugar, dissolved in one cup fresh milk. Boil ten minutes, slowly, still stirring. If the child has fever or cannot digest milk, substitute hot water for it.

HOMINY AND MILK. Boil half a cup of small hominy in one scant quart of cold water with a pinch of salt for one hour, stirring often. While hot, mix till soft with new milk, sweeten to taste, and feed to the baby with a spoon. This is relaxing to the child's bowels and should not be given if the child is disposed to summer complaint.

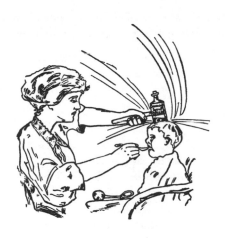

Soothing syrups are poisons to babies.
They contain opium. Opium kills babies.
Don't dope your baby.

GRAHAM HASTY PUDDING. Stir one cup of Graham flour, wet up with cold water, into one large cup boiling water with one teaspoon of salt. Boil ten minutes, stirring almost constantly. Add one large cup milk and cook, after it has come again to a boil, ten minutes longer. Give with sugar and milk for breakfast. Eaten with cream, nutmeg, and powdered sugar, this is a good plain dessert for grown people as well as children.

MILK PORRIDGE. Wet to a paste one tablespoon Indian meal in one cup cold white flour water. Boil the paste in two cups boiling water with a good pinch of salt for 20 minutes; add two cups milk and cook ten minutes more, stirring often. Eat with sugar and milk, stirred in while hot.

Prescriptions for Sound Sleep

PROVIDE SEPARATE SLEEPING ENCLOSURES. Where should infants sleep? Never in bed between the parents. It is especially important that children, after a very early age, should have separate cradles or cribs provided for them and that they be taught to occupy them.

DON'T USE THE OLD-FASHIONED CRADLE. The emanations from the sleeper's lungs and skin should be allowed to escape freely. This is impossible in a close, deep cradle. The crib, with the skeleton sides, is just the thing. If his head is too high at night, round shoulders will result; uneven shoulders result from allowing a child to sleep continually on one side.

USE PROPER BEDDING. The best bed at all seasons of the year is one of oat straw. This is light and soft. It is better than hair, because the straw can often be changed and the tick washed. In cold weather a thick woolen blanket should be doubled and spread over the straw bed to increase the warmth. For covering the little sleeper, woolen blankets should alone be used.

USE PROPER PILLOWS. The pillow as well as the bed should be of straw. The heads of American children are for the most part little furnaces! Much mischief comes from keeping them buried in feather pillows 20 hours out of 24. I have seen scores of babies die of brain maladies, who would have recovered if their brains had not been baked in feather pillows.

ESTABLISH ROUTINE BED TIMES. Let the care be to establish an hour for retiring, so early that their fullest sleep may be out before sunrise. After ten o'clock at night, the old, the middle-aged, and the young should be in bed; and the early rising will take care of itself, with the incalculable accompaniment of a fully rested body and a renovated brain.

ATTEND HIM AT BED TIME. Give him light suppers and put him to bed early in a dark room. See that his feet are warm, his stomach easy, and his body not overloaded with blankets and quilts; also, that the nursery is clean amid freshly aired. He will not grow better in a glare of artificial light than will your camellias and azaleas.

MAKE CLOTHES FOR SLEEPING. Children should not wear the same garment next to the skin at night that they have worn through the day. If the nightgown is worn more than one night without going to the wash-room, it should be hung up to be thoroughly aired during the day, and if possible in the sun.

AVOID EXCESSIVE EVENING STIMULATION. Certainly it would be unwise to excite young children by too much conversation with them just before putting them to bed. All study should be forbidden in the evening for children who have difficulty going to sleep.

MOTHER, YOU MUST PUT HIM TO BED. There are some mothers who think it a self denial to leave the parlors, firesides, or work, to put their little children to bed. They think that the nurse could do it just as well; that it is of no consequence who hears the children say their prayers. Now, putting aside the pleasure of opening the little bed and tucking the darling up, there are really important reasons why the mother should not yield this privilege to any other. In the first place, it is the time of all times when a child is inclined to show its confidence and affection. But of this all mothers may be assured, that the last words at night are of great importance, even to the babies of the flock; the very tones of the voice they last listened to make an impression on their sensitive organizations. Mother, do not think the time and strength wasted that you spend in reviewing the day with your little boy or girl. It has had its disappointments and trials as well as its play and pleasures; it is ready to throw its arms around your neck and take its good-night kiss.

What a mother sings to the cradle goes all the way down to the coffin.

—Henry Ward Beecher (1813–1887)
President, Ohio's Lane Theological Seminary

ASSURE ADEQUATE VENTILATION. An intelligent mother, having acquainted herself with the principles of ventilation, will not retire to her own room for the night without having provided a sufficiency of air for her own children in the same manner that she provides and regulates their night covering or any other requisite for refreshing slumber.

PRAY WITH THEM. Pray with the child in simple and earnest language it can understand. The following beautiful little prayer is said to have been composed and used by a boy 13 years old:

Father, now the day is past, on thy child thy blessing cast;
Near my pillow hand in hand, keep thy guardian angel band;
And throughout the darkling night bless me with a cheerful light.
Let me rise at morn again, free from every care and pain;
Pressing through life's thorny way, keep me, Father, day by day.

Rules for Parents

DO NOT LET SERVANTS STAND IN YOUR PLACE. That children are so much left to the care of servants in so many families of the middle classes is, perhaps, in many cases unavoidable. Nevertheless, it is a great evil. It has been observed that children who are attended to by their mother, who are undressed and put to bed by her, who open their eyes in the morning to behold her cheerful eyes and loving looks, who by her are dressed and kept under her judicious care throughout the day are, as a rule, far more good-tempered, healthy, and intelligent than such as are left almost wholly to the care of servants.

FATHERS, BE WITH THEM. The father who plunges into business so deeply that he has no leisure for domestic pleasures and whose only intercourse with his children consists in a brief word of authority or a surly lamentation is to be both pitied and blamed.

SET FOR THEM EXAMPLES. Mother, Father, be what the children ought to be. Do what the children ought to do. Avoid what they should avoid. Think well that those by whom you are surrounded are often only the reflection of yourself. Are any among them defective? Examine what you are yourself, what you avoid—in a word, your whole conduct. Do you discover in yourself defects, sins, wandering? Begin by improving yourself and seek afterward to improve your children. The hearthstone must be the shrine of purity, of generous teachings, the repository of the virtues. In its shelter are taught those lessons that make the girls and boys who go from its walls good women and men who will leave their impress upon the world.

Teach Them Well while You Have Them

There are few who can receive the honors of a college, but all are graduates of the hearth.

CULTIVATE THEIR MENTAL POWERS. Parents have been warned of late that a child with a precocious brain or who is very forward, to use the common expression, is more liable to dangerous diseases of the brain than other children and that indulging their precocious appetites will increase the excitement of the brain and result in inflammation and premature death. Parents have, therefore, been urged to retard the education of the mental powers. But modern mental science acknowledges that we may begin at a very early period to work upon the conceptive and perceptive faculties, not only without danger, but with manifest advantage, for very early life is the proper period for the expansion of these faculties.

TEACH TRUTHFULNESS BY YOUR OWN EXAMPLE. The child's sense of the deep heinousness of falsehood must be strengthened by example. The reverence for truth may be increased by the sight of truth-loving and truth-practicing parents. If parents realized how great was their responsibility, how closely they were watched and copied, they would place a perpetual guard upon their lips and manners.

GUIDE THEM TOWARD PURE COMPANIONS. Show them how to select those for intimates who will not lower their moral tone. We do not refer to their social position; many a poor boy is an innate gentleman. Teach your children so that they will shrink from contact with the coarse and impure and will not choose their companions for the money they possess, but for their worth and manners.

ALLOW THEM CHOICE OF THEIR OWN OCCUPATIONS. When children reach a certain age, they begin to consider what pursuit they shall engage in. It is unwise to bias the mind of the young in this matter. Whatever their natural tastes incline them to should become their life work. The majority of parents decide these questions for their children, dissatisfaction arises, and continually they feel that they are misplaced. Watch the bent of the young minds; converse with them as to their predilections. They will learn any business more readily if they are interested in it.

Teach Them Independence. All children should cherish a desire to do all they can for themselves and to support themselves by their labor as early as possible. Those who lean on father and mother for everything will find it hard work to get along by and by, as they may have to do when their parents die. Those who early learn to rely upon themselves will have little difficulty in earning their own living.

Teach Daughters the Lessons of the Home. No matter your daughter's position in her father's home, in our country of variable fortunes, there is no insurance against her compulsion into the kitchen for her daily bread, once she is a wife. The time may not come when the daughters of wealth shall be obliged to take their stand in the kitchen, but should they not know how to bake and wash? We shall never have good puddings and pies, chowders and fricassees, while the ladies are taught that it is a disgrace to learn to cook. Teach them how to make bread as well as rick-rack. If they show a talent for music, give them a chance, but not before they can broil a steak or make a decent cup of coffee.

Teach Sons to Earn Their Own. Many an unwise parent labors hard and lives sparingly for the purpose of giving his children a start in the world, as it is called. Instead of striving to lay up fortunes for your son, teach him the habits of business and so give him treasures more staple than stocks and bonds. Setting a young man afloat with money left by relatives is like tying bladders under the arms of one who cannot swim; ten chances to one he will lose his bladders and go to the bottom. Teach him to swim.

Teach Them These Rules for Deportment:

- *Respect for others.* Teach them to respect each other's rights—to enjoy their merry romp and innocent fun without hurting each other's feelings or playing upon some weakness.
- *Obedience.* Let us acknowledge the habit of obedience to be the primary virtue. The first lesson a child should be taught is filial respect and a deferent yielding of its own wishes to those of its parents. This does not imply a slavish submission or a crushing out of individuality. It means that the tie between parent and child should be so strong and the confidence so great that there would be no chance for the clashing of will.
- *Courtesy.* Children must not be allowed to have two sets of manners, one for home use and the other for company. They can be taught to exercise gentle manners at home, to be thoughtful of the comfort of every member of the family and to be guilty of no act that they would blush for were other eyes upon them. Then they will become real gentlemen or ladies.
- *Respect for elders.* Teach them to be deferent to those who are their superiors in age and position. "Young America" has the idea that it is a proof of independence and manliness to speak flippantly and sneeringly of parents or guardians, referring to them as "the governor," "the old lady," or "the old party." There is no greater mistake made.
- *Order.* Teach them to have certain places for their clothes, toys, tools, and books; and when they are done using them, to put them in their place.
- *Fairness.* Teach them to be fair in play, and not to cheat. This may be a hard lesson to learn, but it is one of the grandest.
- *Respect for others' belongings.* Tell them never meddle with other people's property. As a rule, it is very offensive to have one's cherished articles handled indiscriminately.
- *Silence.* It is very rude for children to ask direct questions, such as "Where are you going?'" or "What have you got in that package?" In fact, they should not show curiosity about other people's affairs.

- ※ *Modesty*. Modesty among boys and girls is as highly appreciated as among grown people, and a young person who ventures to think himself a little better than his associates can hardly help carrying the thought into action. By such conduct he makes himself exceedingly disagreeable.

- ※ *Manners*. Many children form habits which are not nice, such as spitting on the floor, scratching the head, stretching themselves out upon a chair, and yawning. All such habits are exceedingly low-bred and should be avoided.

- ※ *Succinctness*. If they have occasion to enter a place of business, train your children to state what they want and then retire as quickly as possible. They have no right to encroach upon the time of a man of business.

The Proper Use of Praise and Punishment

There are two great motives influencing human action—hope and fear. Both of these are at times necessary. But who would not prefer to have her child influenced to good conduct by a desire of pleasing rather than by the fear of offending?

TEMPER THEM EARLY. Like steel we all need to be tempered; otherwise, weak or brittle will be our wills; and this tempering process should commence even in infancy. As the child, so the man or woman. If we allow our little ones to express spite or malice in vindictive ways we cannot hope the fault will annihilate itself as they grow older.

UNDERSTAND AND REASON WITH THEM. The fear of ridicule, pain, and shame drives children into falsehoods. Lies caused by dread of punishment may be avoided if it is understood that a child guilty of wrong should be forgiven if he made a straightforward, honest acknowledgment of the same. Children are very delicate instruments. Men play upon them as if they were tough as drums and, like drums, made for beating. Do not terrorize them, but reason gently and plainly with them. One in sympathy with their little souls will lead them along safely amid temptations to falsehood.

APPRECIATE, RESPECT, AND TRUST THEM. Show the young people of your household that you respect their efforts and aid them with your riper judgment, and they will strive harder to be worthy of the trust you put in them. As flowers cannot grow without sunlight, neither can the young thrive unless they are treated with consideration and assistance. Parents who never have a word of praise for their children, who deny a bit of approval or a welcoming smile to their own, are chilling the warmest feelings of the heart. They are withering the bright blossoms of love and confidence, which cannot live without careful nurture.

Fear secretes acids; but love and trust are sweet juices.

—Henry Ward Beecher (1813–1887)
President, Ohio's Lane Theological Seminary

PUNISH CONSISTENTLY. Let your punishments be constant, direct, unhesitating, and not to be escaped; the punishment need not and should not be severe, just enough to let the sensitive heart of the child understand that mother is displeased. I think you will find that, by this method, you reduce the punishment you would otherwise be compelled to inflict, for you soon secure a habit of obedience, after which punishments will be almost unnecessary.

REFRAIN FROM FAULTFINDING. Scolding, finding fault, and recrimination are even below the dignity of punishment. Nothing will rasp and embitter the soul more deeply than a railing, "nagging" tongue. Mothers often fall into the habit of chiding their children for every little offense. It is "Don't do this and don't do that," from morning until night. The command becomes odious to the child, and he pays as little attention to his mother's remonstrance as to a cat's mew.

ADMINISTER PUNISHMENT WITH SELF POSSESSION. If done in a towering passion, punishment takes the character of revenge, and the child resists it with defiance, stubbornness, or a feeling of being injured. Place clearly before the child the nature of the aggravation and that the sole design of the chastisement is his present and future welfare.

Never correct a child by scolding, admonition, or castigation in the presence of any person whatever. It is an attack on its self esteem, which provokes resistance and passion and arouses a rebellious spirit which often breaks out in open defiance or sullen resentment.

SPEAK GENTLY. I know some houses in which sharp, angry tones resound from morning till night, and the influence is as contagious as measles and much more to be dreaded in a household. The children catch it and it lasts for life, an incurable disease.

Some Advice for Playtime

We had a charming Thanksgiving dinner in the state dining room. All the executive clerks and their wives and little folks were our guests. One roast pig and three turkeys (one a monster from Rhode Island, Governor Van Zant). After a happy dinner from 2:30 to 5 p.m., blindman's buff gave entertainment to the little folks.

> —Rutherford B. Hayes
> Diary entry, A White House
> Thanksgiving, November 29, 1878

LET THEM MAKE THEIR OWN. Playthings that the children make for themselves are a great deal better than those which are bought for them. A little girl had better fashion her cups and saucers of acorns than to have a set of earthen ones supplied.

MAKE HER A DOLL. For the wee little girl, make a nice rag doll; it will please her as well as a boughten one; and, besides, that sort of a dollie can be handled ever so roughly without any danger of breaking its neck or limbs.

SEND THEM OUT. The truth is that "all out doors," as the phrase is, is the only proper apartment for them. A child brought up in the city, accustomed only to the limitations of a daily walk, is really defrauded of its childhood; and, what is more mournful, the theft can never be atoned for in after life. Nothing can make up for it, for the gleeful delight of picking shells upon the seashore, or plucking a handful of flowers wheresoever it chooses to stray, or looking at the animal creation, every one of which, from a caterpillar to an ox, is a marvel and wonder compared to which a toy shop is of no interest whatever.

TAKE YOUR BABY OUT, TOO. A baby can no more flourish in the dark than a flower. Like the flower, it needs sunshine. Do not fear its eyes will be injured if the sun shine in its face; and when you take it out to ride, unless the sun is coming down strong, do not cover up its face with the carriage top.

Baby outdoors

GARDEN WITH THEM. Encourage the children in gardening by giving them a corner, "all for their own" and some seeds to put in it. Show them how to make beds and take care of them; tell them how the flowers grow and always encourage them to watch and study them in their development. Such employment will keep them out of a great deal of mischief. There are no safer companions than flowers.

MAKE FUN IN THE WORK OF THE HOME. A toy flatiron is sold that is not only useful in the hands of a child for ironing dolls' clothes but also as a lesson in domestic economy.

Chapter Three

Caring for a Sick Family Member

During the Illness

Provide Circulation. Pure air is of vital importance in the sick room. Many persons exclude fresh air for fear of dampness, but even damp air is better than impure. Even in cold weather, there should be a free circulation of air. In summer it is often more important to keep hot air out than to let cool air in.

Keep Up a Fire. The sight of a bright blaze is calculated to cheer the patient, while the sight of a dark, close stove is depressing. By no means allow a sick person to be in a room warmed by a flue or register.

Manage Odors. It is best to have no odors in the sick-room unless it be bay rum, German cologne, or something else especially fancied by the sick person. Cologne water will not dispel a foul odor, while disinfectants are noisome in themselves. When there is any unpleasant exhalation, it is far better to let it escape by properly ventilating the room than to try to overcome it by the aid of perfumery. In fevers, where there are offensive exhalations from the body, sponging with tepid water will help to remove the odor, and will also prove soothing to the patient.

A careful consumptive—not dangerous to live with:

1. Coughs, spits, and sneezes into paper or cloth;
2. burns or boils it before it dries,
3. or puts it into a disinfectant.
4. Washes her hands before and afer eating.
5. Always uses the same dishes and boils them in water before washing other dishes.
6. Sleeps alone.

In case of consumtion look to these for cure:

1. The doctor.
2. Sunlight.
3. Outdoor air.
4. Good food.
5. Rest.

TAKE CARE HIS SENSITIVITIES. Do not keep the medicines where he can see them, nor ever let him witness the mixing of that which he is to swallow. As soon as his meals are over, remove every vestige of them from the room. Even a soiled spoon, lying on table or bureau, may offend his fastidious appetite. Cover the stand or waiter from which he eats with a spotless napkin, and serve his food in your daintiest ware.

WELCOME THE SUN FOR THEM. Cases are not rare in which invalids have been restored to health by using sun baths and otherwise freely enjoying the sunshine.

TAKE CARE OF THE LINENS. Be careful to keep warm, soft flannels on the sick person in winter. In summer, do not keep a pile of bed-clothes on the patient, even if chilly. It is better to keep up the circulation by other means, such as rubbing or stimulants. Scrupulous neatness should be observed about the bed linen. Use soft, fleecy blankets. The nurse should watch her opportunity of having the bed-clothes taken into the fresh air and shaken and the bed made up when the patient has been lifted up and set in an easy-chair near the fire.

FOLLOW DOCTOR'S ORDERS. First of all, after a reliable physician has been called in, his directions should be strictly followed, and his instructions should be the law in the sick room. Have everything in readiness for his admission immediately after his arrival, as his time is valuable and it occasions him annoyance and loss of time to be kept waiting outside of the sick room after reaching the house of the patient.

KEEP HIM CHEERED. The patient should be indulged in every fancy that is not hurtful. Study all pleasant and soothing arts to while away the time and keep worry of every kind away from him.

ARRANGE A DRIVE. Driving out is a delightful recreation for convalescents, and they should be indulged in it as soon as the physician pronounces it safe. In winter, they should be carried driving about noon so as to enjoy the sunshine at its warmest. In summer, the cool of the morning or evening is the best time to drive them out; but, if the latter time be chosen, be careful to return immediately after sundown. It is well to have some little refreshment awaiting after the drive.

DO NOT ADMIT VISITORS. In a case of illness, many well-meaning persons crowd to see the patient. Do not admit them into the sick room, as it is too exciting and fatiguing to an ill person to see company; and, when in a critical condition, the balance might be disastrously turned by the injudicious admission of visitors.

Take Care How You Feed Your Charge

SEASON AND HEAT MODERATELY. It must be remembered that the palate is more sensitive in sickness than in health, both to seasonings and temperatures, so that less seasoning and more moderate degrees of heat must be observed.

USE DELICACY IN PREPARATION. As the sick are very fastidious, all foods for them must be prepared in the most delicate manner. Have all hot beverages brought to the door of the sick room in a covered pitcher, then poured into the cup, thus avoiding the danger of spilling liquids into the saucer while carrying them to the patient.

GIVE SMALL PORTIONS. A big bowl of broth or jelly will either tempt him to imprudence or discourage him. "Am I to be burdened with all that?" cries the affrighted stomach, and will have none of it. For this reason it is preferable to serve small portions and present the meal by courses rather than place all on the tray at one time.

ASSIST IF NECESSARY. While he is weak, feed him with your own hand and talk cheerily of something besides his food and coax him into taking the needed nutriment as only a wife and mother can.

VARY THE LOCATION OF SERVICE. Those who have suffered from long sickness know the loathing attendant upon the idea that all food is tainted with the atmosphere in which it is served and, if eaten in bed, tastes of the mattress and pillows.

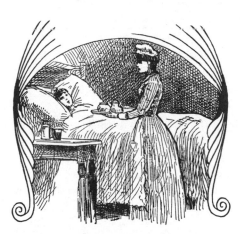

Food for the sick

VARY THE FOOD'S INCARNATIONS. When the dietary is limited, serve the foods that are permitted in as many forms as possible. For instance, beef tea may be given hot in the form of beef essence, as savory jelly, frozen, and as beef tea custard.

After the Illness

FUMIGATE. The sick room in all cases and preferably every room in the house, in case of smallpox, diphtheria, typhoid and other virulent diseases, should be thoroughly disinfected by fumigation. This may be accomplished by formaldehyde gas or by the fumes of burning sulphur.

DISINFECT THE ROOM. After the sick room has been fumigated with formaldehyde or sulphur, thoroughly wash the floor and woodwork and all out of the way places—window ledges, picture moulding—and thoroughly wet all dust and dirt in cracks with the half-strength Standard Solution No. 3, Bichloride of Mercury. Follow this up with hot soap suds; afterwards rinse with cloths wet in the disinfectant. Do not attempt to mix soap with the disinfectant solution. Scrape and burn the wallpaper. Wipe the ceiling and walls before repapering and open the room to sunlight and air for several days. Apply a fresh coat of paint to the woodwork. Burn all books, magazines, newspapers and other articles the value of which is not great enough to warrant disinfection. No person should enter the sick room until it has been thoroughly disinfected.

CHANGE OR DISINFECT BEDDING. Throw straw beds out of the window, empty out and burn the straw, and disinfect the tick as for cotton clothing. Disinfect feather beds, pillows, quilts, comforters, and blankets in a steam disinfector when practical, or if not soiled, with formaldehyde in large quantities. If mattresses have been soiled by the patient's discharges and steaming disinfection is not practical, burn them.

PART FOUR

Meal Preparation

CHAPTER ONE

SETTING YOURSELF TO THE TASK

Method, skill, and economy in the kitchen may safely be styled the root, the foundation, of housewifery.

Going to Market

As the excellence of a dinner depends as much upon the quality of its materials as upon the skill of the cook, it is incumbent on the good housekeeper to have some knowledge of marketing. The skilled marketer must have experience, but even the youngest beginner can gain some advantage from such clear and explicit description as is presented here.

CHOOSE THE FRESHEST INGREDIENTS. The least taint in any ingredient will impair the flavor of the dish and often produce temporary discomfort or positive illness; therefore, the marketer should not be tempted to purchase wilted vegetables or meat because the price may be low.

TRY MANY CUTS OF MEAT. It is a favorite maxim among good old-fashioned housekeepers that only prime cuts of meat are of good value. But this is the case only when the family taste insists always upon a

roast or a steak; when any variety of fare is acceptable, many of the cheap cuts can be made into delicious dishes. As a matter of fact, most of the edible viscera can be made into palatable and nutritious dishes; and some of the so-called cheap cuts of meat are preferable, on the score of flavor and strength-giving properties, to the most expensive.

BE FAMILIAR WITH THE QUALITIES OF GOOD MEAT. The best meats are from well-fed, mature animals which have not been overworked and the meat of which has been carefully transported from the slaughterhouse to the market. While the flesh of young meats seems thus relatively tender, it is not so acceptable to the palate as that of mature animals in good condition. This is the reason why such young meats as veal and suckling pig are not desirable foods for persons whose digestion is impaired. Good meat has very little smell and diffuses a certain medicinal odor. Bad meat has the peculiarity that it shrinks considerably in the boiling; wholesome meat rather swells and does not lose an ounce in weight.

RELY ON THE DEALER FOR GAME. Prime game is clean, fat, and free from any unpleasant or musty odor. The most abundant is venison; but buffalo, bear, elk, antelope, wild sheep and goat, rabbits, hares, squirrels, raccoons, otters, beavers, and badgers are marketed. With all game, the judgment of a reliable dealer is the best guide for the buyer.

CHOOSE GAME BIRDS CAREFULLY. Game birds are abundant in all parts of America, in their season, and can usually be bought in good condition from reliable dealers. The breasts should always be full and tender and skin upon the rump and about the vent clear and freshly colored; if there is any appearance of discoloration, the birds are stale. A few feathers plucked from these parts will disclose the color of the skin, and a touch will indicate the condition of the breast. Despite the fact that epicures like game hung until it is upon the verge of putrefaction, it is neither safe nor wholesome food in that condition.

SELECT FRESH, SEASONAL FISH AND SEAFOOD. Look for full, bright eyes, clean skin, and firm flesh in fish. Above all, the odor should be sweet and fresh. Sea fish have the finest flavor; freshwater fish sometimes have a muddy taste, which can be removed to some extent by soaking in salted cold water for a couple of hours before cooking. Good crabs and lobsters are heavy in proportion to their size, and, while uncooked, their movements are rapid; if cooked, their odor is sweet. Choose the smallest plump oysters which can be obtained. The shells of mussels in good condition are dark and bright, and the fish fills them plumply; the edges of the shells are sharp and firmly closed. Cod, whitefish, striped bass, smelts, blackfish, flounder, and halibut will be found all the year round; bluefish through June, July, and August; mackerel through spring and summer; and Spanish mackerel from June to October.

CHOOSE FULL, FRESH VEGETABLES. All juicy and green vegetables should be very fresh and succulent and are best just before flowering, as also are the sweet herbs called pot herbs. Roots and tubers should be full and fresh-colored; if withered or sprouted, they are inferior. The green vegetables should not be bought in larger quantity than can be used while they are still fresh; they will keep best if sprinkled with water and laid in a cool, dark place. All the roots and tubers are improved by laying them in cold water for an hour before using them.

CONSIDER TIME OF USE WHEN PURVEYING FRUIT. Fruit when fresh should be ripe and sound, as perfect as possible (because this will make less waste), and bought only in quantities that admit speedy use, although winter fruit can be kept without any danger of spoiling. Preserved and dried fruits keep well in cool, dark places and so may be bought safely in quantities.

PURCHASE DAIRY IN SMALL QUANTITIES. Milk, butter, cheese, and eggs are so perishable that it is not well to purchase them in quantities larger than required for a few days' use, unless the family is large and can consume such amounts as are sold at wholesale prices.

BUY DRY GOODS IN BULK. Corn and wheat products, and cereals in general, may be bought by large quantity if there is a good dry storeroom where they can be secured from destructive vermin and mold.

Advice on Setting Yourself to the Task

We may as well start from the right point, if we hope to continue, friends. You must definitely learn the rudiments of the art of meal preparation for yourself. Practice, and practice alone, will teach you certain essentials.

REMEMBER CLEANLINESS. The last thing you should do before beginning to cook is to wash your hands and clean your nails.

PREPARE INGREDIENTS. Prepare each ingredient for mixing, that the dish may not be delayed when half finished because the flour is not sifted, the "shortening" not warmed, the sugar and butter not creamed, the meat not cut up, or the herbs not minced.

SAVE FAILURES FOR YOURSELF. Scorched soups and custards, sour bread, biscuit yellow with soda, and cake heavy as lead come under the head of "hopeless." They are absolutely unfit to be set before civilized beings and educated stomachs. Should such mishaps occur, lock the memory of the attempt in your own bosom, and do not vex or amuse your guests with the narration, still less with visible proof of the calamity.

Bad dinners go hand in hand with total depravity, while a properly fed man is already half saved.

> —The Women of the First Congregational Church,
> Marysville, Ohio, 1876
> *Centennial Buckeye Cook Book*

DO NOT APOLOGIZE. Many a partial failure would pass unobserved but for the clouded brow and earnest apologies of the hostess. Do not apologize except at the last gasp! You will be astonished to find, if you keep your wits about you, how often even your husband will remain in blissful ignorance that aught has gone wrong if you do not tell him. You know so well what should have been the product of your labor that you exaggerate the justice of others' perceptions.

I do not like to cook. I hate fussing with food. . . . I'd rather go hungry than broil a steak or boil potatoes. I love business.

> —Mrs. Warren G. Harding
> *The Misanthrope's Corner: Personal Look at President Warren Harding's Wife Florence Harding,*
> National Review, October 26, 1998

PRESENT A VARIETY OF DISHES. The least pampered palate will weary of stereotyped bills of fare. Never risk the success of your entire meal upon a new dish; have something which you know your husband can eat and introduce experiments as by-play. But do not be too shy of innovations in the shape of untried dishes. Variety is not only pleasant but healthful. It is an idea which should have been exploded long ago that plain roast Monday through Thursday, cod on Friday, and pork-and-beans every Saturday, because economical, are means of grace.

We in America have the raw material of provision in greater abundance than any other nation. There is no country where an ample, well-furnished table is more easily spread . . .

> —Harriet Beecher Stowe
> *House and Home Papers,* 1869

Advice on Using Recipes

LEARN TO COOK NO MATTER YOUR CIRCUMSTANCES. For those who will only oversee the cooking, teach yourselves, nevertheless. As one wife relayed: "When I took possession of my first real home, five good friends presented me with as many cookbooks, each complete

A coat of melted lard

and all by different compilers. One day's investigation of my menage convinced me that my lately hired servants either knew no more about cookery than I did or affected stupidity to develop my capabilities or ignorance. Too proud to let them suspect the truth or to have it bruited abroad as a topic for pitying or contemptuous gossip, I shut myself up with my "Complete Housewives" and inclined seriously to the study of the same, comparing one with the other and seeking to shape a theory which should grow into practice in accordance with the best authority."

LEARN BY DOING. I'll not forget the advice of a dear friend who lifted me up from despondency when I was early married. "Bless your innocent little heart!" she cried, in her fresh, gay voice. "Ninety-nine out of a hundred cookbooks are written by people who never kept house, and the hundredth by a good cook who yet doesn't know how to express herself to the enlightenment of others. Compile a recipe book for yourself. Make haste slowly. Learn one thing at a time, and when you have mastered it, make a note of it, never losing sight of the principle that you must do it in order to learn how."

TAKE LIBERTIES WITH RECIPES. In the matter of seasoning and other minor details, consult your judgment and your husband's taste. Take this liberty with whatever recipe you think you can improve.

CHAPTER TWO

COOKING METHODS, TERMS, AND MEASUREMENTS

Cooking Methods

Whatever the manner chosen for dressing food, it can be traced to one of the comparatively few fundamental methods of cookery. If the fact is once accepted that in cookery similar results follow definite operations as certainly as they do in any other manual work, there need be no uncertainty or failure.

FIRST, LEARN TO MANAGE A FIRE. You must know how to manage a fire, for if you fail in that you will fail in your cooking; therefore, you must understand all about the dampers, and in buying a stove one should learn at the shop how and when to open and close them. When you start your fire the dampers should all be open. Do not lay paper flat in the fire basket, but twist it in bunches, putting in first the paper, then kindlings, so crossed as to let the air draw through, placing the heavier pieces of wood upon the top. As soon as all are well burning, add two or three shovelfuls of coal. It is better to feed the fire often at first, but by the time you are ready to cook it must be a solid fire. Methods include:

⟶ *Deep frying.* The frying of fish balls, doughnuts, and other foods should be done in a deep frying pan or round-bottomed kettle called a Scotch bowl, half full of drippings, lard, butter, or olive oil, at choice. Olive oil is the best medium for frying fish of any kind. The fat must be placed over the fire until a thin smoke begins to rise from its surface; at that temperature, its heat will crisp the outside of any food put into it, and so prevent that soaking of fat which renders some fried foods so unwholesome. As soon as the fried article is browned to the desired degree and floats upon the surface of the hot fat, remove it with a skimmer, lay it upon brown paper to free it from grease, and serve it at once.

Boiling. Boiling consists of immersing any article in actually boiling water and maintaining the temperature of the water at the boiling point until the article is cooked.

Stewing and simmering. Stewing and simmering consist of first bringing any article of food to the boiling point in water or sauce and then continuing the cooking at a very gentle rate of boiling until the food is done. These kinds of boiling make food very tender and digestible and prepare its properties for immediate and complete nutrition; they are invaluable in treating tough meats.

Steaming. Steaming is an excellent way of cooking, calculated to prepare food for imparting all its nutriment to the system. It preserves all the flavor of food and prevents absorption of water when this is undesirable.

Braising. Braising consists of cooking any article of food in water or sauce in a braising pan. This pan may be either round or oval, with a flat bottom and a depressed cover made to hold hot coals or ashes. Braising is used when cooking is done over an open fire, the vessel used being called a bake kettle or old-fashioned Dutch oven. The same effect may be produced by putting a covered saucepan containing food into a moderately hot oven.

Gilding. Gilding is covering any surface of food with the beaten yolk of a raw egg, and subsequently drying or browning it in the oven. Fancy pastry is generally gilded.

Larding. Larding, a great improvement to retain moisture and add richness, is the insertion of small, even-size strips of fat salt pork, tongue, truffles, or any chosen substance upon the surface of meat, poultry, fish, or game by means of a little split cylinder of steel called a larding needle. This pin, sharp at one end and cleft into four divisions at the other, may be obtained at any hardware store. The lardoons are inserted in the open end of the needle, which is then passed under about half an inch of the surface of the substance to be larded; when the needle is withdrawn, the lardoon remains, both ends projecting slightly. The lardoons are inserted in diagonal lines, the ends of the second line coming between the ends of the first, and so alternating until all the lardoons are used; or they are placed to resemble the stitch in needlework called herringbone.

Daubing. Daube is a French term referring to the insertion of a large lardoon with the grain of the meat through its entire substance, the ends of the lardoon projecting about an inch. In this country, butchers frequently daube beef for a dish called beef à la mode and call the operation larding.

Barding. Barding is fastening over the breast of a bird of any kind a large thin slice of fat salt pork, which in cooking serves the purpose of basting.

Terms

One reason why there is so much uncertainty about American cookery is because many housekeepers modify a standard dish according to their own ideas and then retain the original name. If they have the ability to improve upon an accepted method, they ought to name their dish so as to give it individuality, as justly as inventors who improve upon a patent announce the changes by a new name. Thus, the following proper definitions of dishes and procedures are offered:

- *A la Creole.* Cooked with tomatoes, onions and peppers.
- *A la Printanière.* A soup or stew served with young spring vegetables.
- *Aspic.* A savory jelly for meats, fish, vegetables and salads. Frequently used as a garnish.
- *Au Gratin.* Cooked with browned crumbs and usually with grated cheese.

- *Bechamel.* A rich white sauce made with stock, milk or cream.
- *Bisque.* A thick white sauce or soup generally made from shell-fish.
- *Blanch.* To whiten by scalding.
- *Bouillon.* A meat broth.
- *Bombe.* Molded ices having the outside one variety and the center another.
- *Canapé.* A finger strip of bread or toast spread with a savory compound, usually either fish or egg, daintily garnished and served as an appetizer before lunch or dinner.
- *Collops.* A slice or morsel of meat for stewing; a small portion of anything.
- *Compote.* A dish of fruits cooked in syrup.
- *Croustades.* Small pieces of bread fried or toasted. Used as a garnish for minced or hashed meat.
- *En Brochette.* Small portions of meal, such as chicken livers, cooked with bacon on a skewer.
- *Farci.* Stuffed.
- *Fondue.* Cheese and eggs cooked together.
- *Force-meat.* Finely chopped, highly seasoned meat, served separately or used as a stuffing.
- *Frappé.* Half frozen.
- *Hors d'œuvres.* Small dishes served during the first course of a dinner.
- *Hyson tea.* A green tea from China having a special twist.
- *Isinglass.* Gelatin made from bladders of certain fishes.
- *Jardinière.* Mixed vegetables.
- *Macédoine.* A mixture of vegetables or fruits.
- *Marinate.* To make savory in a mixture of seasonings: oil and vinegar, or oil and lemon juice.
- *Meringue.* White of egg and sugar beaten together.

- *Mousse.* May be savory or sweet. A light, frothy mixture thickened with gelatin with a whisk till spongy in texture and then packed in ice and salt for three or four hours.

- *Mulligatawny.* A rich soup flavored with curry.

- *Pâté.* A small pastry shell, usually made from puff paste. May contain either a sweet or savory filling.

- *Purée.* Meats, vegetables, fish, etc., cooked in liquid till tender, then passed through a sieve.

- *Roux.* A cooked mixture of butter and flour for thickening soups, sauces, and gravies.

- *Rusk.* A light, sweetened bread or biscuit, bread or cake that has been crisped and browned in the oven, then often pounded fine to be eaten with milk.

- *Salmi.* A rich stew of game, half roasted and then cut up and cooked in a sauce.

- *Sauté.* To cook till brown in a shallow pan with a little fat.

- *Soufflé.* Puffed up and made light by use of well-beaten eggs. May be savory or sweet.

- *Suet.* The fatty tissue about the loins and kidneys of sheep, oxen, etc., used in cookery and for making tallow.

- *Sweet bread.* The thymus or pancreas of an animal, used for food, the thymus, being throat sweet bread or sweet bread, the pancreas being stomach sweet bread.

- *Syllabub.* A dish made by mixing wine or cider with milk, forming a soft curd.

- *Tallow.* Animal fat.

- *Terrapin.* Turtle or tortoise, living in fresh or brackish water, highly valued as food.

- *Truss.* To fasten as with skewers or twine, as with a fowl before cooking.

- *Vol-au-vent.* A very light case of puff paste in which savories or sweets may be served.

Household Measures

Butter	When soft, 1 pound is 1 pint.
Powdered white sugar	1 pound 1 ounce are 1 quart.
Best brown sugar	1 pound 2 ounces are 1 quart.
Eggs	10 eggs are 1 pound.
Flour	8 quarts are 1 peck; 4 pecks are 1 bushel.

* 16 large tablespoons are half a pint.
* 8 large tablespoons are 1 gill.
* 2 gills are half a pint.
* A tablespoon is half an ounce.
* 60 drops are equal to a teaspoon.
* 4 teaspoons are equal to 1 tablespoon.

Cook's Measures

* Use a piece the size of a walnut.
* Make it up into balls the size of an orange.
* Use a lump the size of a hen's egg/a guinea egg/a turkey's egg.
* Use a handful.
* Cut in pieces the size of your hand.
* Use a lump as large as your double fist.
* Pat into pones as wide as the wrist.
* Use a pinch.
* Cut in tolerably thick slices.
* Use a heaping plateful.
* Use enough to make it as stiff as soft gingerbread.
* Add brandy, as much as you think best.

Chapter Three

ℙreparing Common Foods

Herein, rather than giving recipes for specific dishes—those come later in the book—I have imparted bits of wisdom earned with experience regarding the general preparation of the foods we most often make. These are the matters often taken for granted by cooks of some years and left out of so many named recipes. These thoughts follow no particular system; they are simply notable observations made during my cooking life.

Bread

When the bread rises in the oven, the heart of the housewife rises with it.

Mrs. Bremer might have added that the heart of the housewife sinks in sympathy with the sinking bread. Bread is so vital an element in our nourishment that I have assigned to it the first place in my work.

Use Good Flour. Good flour is an indispensable requisite to good bread and, next, good yeast and sufficient kneading. Only experience will enable you to be a good judge of flour. One test is to rub the dry flour between your fingers, and if the grains feel round, it is a sign that the flour is good. If after trying a barrel of flour twice, you find it becomes wet and sticky, after being made up of the proper consistency, you had better then return it to your grocer.

Cook's Delight Baking Powder is warranted to make light, sweet, and nutritious food. When good flour is used it has no equal for the immediate production of biscuit, corn bread, rolls, ginger bread, and all kinds of cake, fruits, and dumplings. Cook's Delight may be purchased from R. Brandriff in Piqua, Ohio.

—Advertisement in the
Centennial Buckeye Cook Book, 1876

SUN AND AIR FLOUR BEFORE USE. In the morning, get out the flour to be made up at night for next morning's breakfast. Sift it in a tray and put it out in the sun, or, if the day is damp, set it near the kitchen fire.

USE GOOD YEAST. The best flour is worthless without good yeast. Yeast should be foamy and frothy with a scent slightly like ammonia.

LEARN THE ART OF MIXING. There is a great art in mixing bread, and it is necessary to observe a certain rotation in the process. To make a small quantity of bread, first sift one quart of flour; into that sift a teaspoon of salt; next rub in an Irish potato, boiled and mashed fine; then add a piece of lard the size of a walnut, and next a half teacup of yeast in which three teaspoons of white sugar have been stirred. Then make into a soft dough with lukewarm water or milk. If water is too hot with which you mix your dough, it will kill the yeast. Milk should be scalded and then allowed to cool, as the acid in unscalded milk may sour the bread.

KNEAD STEADILY. Knead without intermission for at least half an hour, by the clock. When none of the dough sticks to your hands you can leave off kneading, but not until then, as rested dough is not nearly so nice. Then place it in a stone crock, greased with lard at the bottom, and set it to rise.

PLAN AROUND RISING TIME. As bread rises much more quickly in summer than in winter, you must make allowance for this difference, during the respective seasons. The whole process, including both the first and second rising, may be accomplished in seven or eight hours in summer, though this will be regulated partly by the flour, as some

Kneading fermented bread dough

kinds of flour rise much more quickly than others. For breakfast, you may make it up at nine o'clock in the evening in summer for an eight o'clock breakfast next morning; but in winter, make it up at seven o' clock. If hot bread is desired for dinner, reserve part of the breakfast dough, keeping it in the kitchen in winter and in the refrigerator in summer till two hours before dinner.

HANDLE DOUGH LIGHTLY. Never knead bread a second time after it rises, as this ruins it. Handle lightly as possible, make into the desired shapes, and put into the molds to be bake. Use a little lard on the hands when making out the loaf or else dip a feather in lard and pass lightly over the bread just before putting it in the oven to bake, so as to keep the crust from being too hard. The top must be pricked so that the crust will not bind. Let it be a little warmer during the second rise than during the first. Always shape and put in the molds two hours before breakfast.

CHECK FOR DONENESS. When the top of the loaf is a light amber color, put back the paper that the bread may not brown too much while thoroughly baking. Turn the mold around so that each part may be exposed to equal heat. Have an empty baking pan on the shelf above the bread to prevent it from blistering. When a broom straw will pass through and come out dry, it is done.

SERVE BREAD PROPERLY. When thoroughly done and taken from the oven, it should be placed on its side or top crust so that the steam can get out of the bottom of the loaf, which is not so hard as the top crust. Then wrap the bread a few moments in a clean, thick, bread towel and send to the table with a napkin over it to be kept on till each person has taken his seat at table.

ADDITIONAL TIPS ON TOASTING. If you have a large family to toast for, you can get on faster if you lay the slices on the rack in the oven to dry a little while the first pieces are being prepared. Toast can be made over a clean grate fire, but it is nicer when held before the fire. In serving dry toast, the slices should not be piled one upon another, but placed edgewise; piling it makes it tough instead of crisp, as the steam cannot escape when piled.

Milk and Butter

USE TWO SETS OF VESSELS. The most exquisite nicety and care must be observed in the management of milk and butter. A housekeeper should have two sets of milk vessels (tin or earthenware, never stoneware, as this is an absorbent). She should never use twice in succession the same milk vessels without having them scalded and aired.

CHURN CAREFULLY. For making butter, strain unskimmed milk into a scalded churn, where the churning is done daily. This will give a sweeter butter and nicer buttermilk than when cream is skimmed and kept for churning, as this sometimes gives a cheesy taste to the butter. Do not let the milk in the churn exceed blood heat. If overheated, the butter will be white and frothy and the milk thin and sour. Churn as soon as the milk is turned. In summer try to churn early in the morning, as fewer flies are swarming then, and the butter can be made much firmer.

SCALD THE CHURN. A stone churn is in some respects more convenient than a wooden churn; but no matter which you use, the most fastidious neatness must be observed. Have the churn scalded and set out to sun as soon as possible after churning.

Print and Refrigerate Correctly. Butter should be printed early in the morning, while it is cool. A plateful for each of the three meals should be placed in the refrigerator ready for use. Do not set butter in a refrigerator with anything else in it but milk, or in a safe with anything but milk. It readily imbibes the flavor of everything near it. After churning, butter should be taken up in what is called a piggin, first scalded and then filled with cold water. With an old-fashioned butter-stick (scalded), wash and press the butter till no water is left. Then add a little salt, finely beaten. I would advise all housekeepers (even those who do not make their own butter) to keep a piggin, a butter-stick, and a pretty butter-print.

Soup

Most Americans, rich and poor, have some kind of soup every day, either for an entire meal or for a first course of a dinner. As making soup is a tedious process, it is best to make enough at once to last several days.

Prepare Stock in Advance. Soups are made with stock, the water in which meat has been boiled. Excellent stock can be made from the scraps and bones, cooked or uncooked, that are left from roasts and beefsteaks; this is the only way of gaining the last bit of nourishment from them. Whether the meat is cooked or uncooked, it should all be cut in small pieces and the bones broken. Stock should be made the day before it is to be used, and the cake of fat which will rise on the top taken off before it is heated over. If you leave the fat on until it is heated, the stock will keep better. Never cook vegetables in with the stock that is not to be used immediately, as the juices from the vegetables will cause it to ferment. Beef shank is most generally used in making nutritious soup. It is best to get this the day before using it and soak it all night in cold, clear water; otherwise, get it as early in the morning as you can.

Use Uncooked Meat for Clear Soups. Meat and bones should be washed thoroughly, but quickly, in hot water before being put on the fire in cold water. Allow one pound of meat and bone to one quart of water in making stock; be particular to keep closely covered, but skim carefully the first part of the cooking. A cup of cold water poured in will make the scum rise freely.

ALWAYS KEEP MEAT WATER. Never throw away water in which any sort of meat has been boiled, as it much better to simmer hash or a stew in this liquor than in water, and it is also invaluable for basting fowls or meats that have not been parboiled. Strain and season just enough for one meal, reserving the rest as foundation for another sort of soup.

Preparing Common Meats and Game

CLEAN MEAT SPARINGLY. When meat is frozen, lay it in cold water to thaw and then cook quickly to prevent its losing its moisture and sweetness. If possible, keep the meat so clean that it will not be necessary to wash it, as water extracts the juices. If you should unfortunately be obliged to use stale meat or poultry, rub it in and out with soda before washing it.

SEASONAL DURATION. Consider season, temperature, and cooking plans when figuring meat's duration. All meats are better in winter for being kept several weeks; it is well, in summer, to keep them as long as you can without danger of their being tainted. Wild meat will keep longer than domestic meat, because of its firm texture. In average temperate weather, clear and dry, meat which has not been frozen will keep the following length of time: veal and pork, one day; lamb, two days; beef and mutton, from three to ten days; large poultry and game birds, from three to six days; small game, from two to five days; and large game, about a week.

THAWING. Meat and game may be kept frozen until thawed out in cold water and speedily used. In warm, muggy weather, and during summer rains, meat exposed to the air spoils quickly; and the conditions of warmth and moisture to which it is exposed are not unlike those which prevail when frozen meat is exposed to the heat of the fire in roasting and baking. The fact should be remembered that meats which have been kept on the ice and are then exposed to the action of a warm atmosphere taint much more quickly than those that have never been iced.

HANGING. Meats should be hung up and covered with thin cloth or fly-screens in a cool, dark place, free from dampness; they should not be laid upon dishes or boards, because the blood which flows from them taints more quickly than the flesh itself. Meats for broiling, roasting, and baking can be hung longer than those to be boiled.

HEED THESE KEEPING TIMES FOR PREPARED MEATS:

* Soak all hams 24 hours before cooking.
* Corn beef must remain packed down in salt for 10 to 12 days before being put in brine; it is fit for use after two weeks under the brine.
* Spiced beef must remain three to four weeks in the wooden box or tub in which it is turned occasionally in the pickle it makes and rubbed with salt.
* Before hanging beef to smoke, it must remain for ten days in the salt, brown sugar, molasses and saltpeter that has been rubbed on it.
* Allow three weeks to prepare cured beef ham for use; let it remain in molasses a day and two nights and in molasses and salt for ten additional days, hang it up to dry for one week, then smoke it a little and keep hanging till used.
* When the weather will admit of it, mutton is better for being kept a few days before cooking.
* Truffle dressing is usually placed in the turkey two days beforehand to impart its flavor to the fowl. A goose must never be eaten the same day it is killed; if the weather is cold, it should be kept a week before using and before cooking should lie several hours in weak salt and water to remove the strong taste.
* Kill young ducks some days before using, or, if obliged to use them the same day as killed, they are better roasted.

Roast Meat before an Open Fire. Use salt, pepper, butter, or lard, and dredge the meat with flour before roasting, but use little salt at first, as it hardens meat to do otherwise. Baste meat frequently to prevent it from hardening on the outside and to preserve the juices. If possible, roast the meat on a spit before a large, open fire, where there is the intense heat required for cooking and the constantly changing current of air necessary to carry away from the meat the fumes of burning fat, which impair its flavor.

Roast Meat in Modern Ovens. Where an open fireplace cannot be obtained, however, the meat may be well roasted in a stove or range. A clear, hot fire should be made. The meat, properly prepared, should be hung in the oven and placed directly in front of the grate containing the fuel; the greatest available heat being required to quickly crisp the surface and thus retain the juices of the meat. The Dutch or tin ovens are generally provided with a movable hook in the top, upon which the meat is hung, and by means of which it can be turned without changing the position of the oven. Some of the ovens are made with an automatic spring that keeps the meat constantly revolving upon the hook and so favors a uniformly brown surface. Mutton, pork, shoat, and veal should be well done, but beef should be cooked rare.

Broil as You Would Roast. The general principles of roasting apply to broiling. The circulation of free air around the meat carries away from it all the smoke arising from the burning fat and the products of combustion from the fire. Meat for broiling should be cut from an inch to an inch and a half thick; the surface should be scraped with the back of a knife to remove sawdust and bone dust, and then wiped with a wet cloth but not washed. When done, serve it at once. Broiled meat deteriorates if left standing near the fire any length of time after it is cooked

Fry or Half-Fry when Broiling is not Possible. Frying proper is performed by entirely immersing any edible substance in enough smoking-hot fat to cover it. Half-frying is a process similar to broiling save that the hot frying pan replaces the fire, and it is sometimes used for steaks and chops. When this kind of frying is properly done, the meat will be juicy, well flavored, and will closely resemble broiled meat. No butter or fat is put into the pan unless the meat is absolutely lean, and then only enough to prevent the burning of the meat. When the frying pan is so hot that it will siss when the meat touches it, put in the meat, and brown it quickly, first upon one side and then upon the other; then finish cooking it to the desired degree and season and serve it.

BAKE MEAT, IF NECESSARY, AT PROPER TEMPERATURES. Baking is not the most desirable way of cooking meat; but ovens are often available when an open fire cannot be reached. It is desirable that the first exposure of meat should be to the greatest obtainable heat, in order to quickly crisp its surface and confine its natural juices. Besides this, meat put into a cool oven will sometimes become tainted before it is cooked. The oven should be too hot to hold a hand in it even for a moment. The heat can be moderated when it has served this purpose.

PREPARE MEAT FOR BAKING. Wipe meat to be baked with a cloth wet in cold water but do not wash or apply salt to cut surfaces until they are brown, because both tend to draw out the juices. Trim off all defective portions. Meat prepared thus will retain its juices so entirely that a rich gravy will flow from it when it is carved. After the meat is brown, it may be seasoned.

BOIL MEAT SLOWLY. In boiling, put on salt meat in cold water, but fresh meat in hot; salt meat requires more water and a longer time to cook than fresh. Boil slowly, removing the scum as it rises. Keep a tea kettle of boiling water at hand to replenish the water in the pot as it boils away. Do not let the meat boil too hard or too long, as this will toughen it and extract the juices. Tough meats and poultry are rendered more tender by putting a little vinegar or a few slices of lemon in the water.

KEEP MEAT FLAVORING ON HAND. As the housekeeper is sometimes hurried in preparing a dish, it will save time and trouble for her to keep on hand a bottle of meat flavoring compounded by putting in a quart bottle and covering with cider vinegar: two chopped onions, three pods of red pepper (chopped), two tablespoons brown sugar, one table-spoon each of celery seed and ground mustard, and one teaspoon each of black pepper and salt. A tablespoon of this mixed in a stew, steak, or gravy will impart not only a fine flavor but a rich color.

Calf

ASK THE BUTCHER TO PREPARE IT SOMEWHAT. Have the butcher to remove the hair by scalding and scraping, to remove the teeth and the eyes from the head, and to split the head in two pieces without cutting the tongue or brains. Likewise, have him split the feet.

REMEMBER AT HOME, FOR CALF, TO:

▦ Thoroughly wash the head in plenty of cold water, carefully scraping the interior of the nasal passage and the mouth. Cover the head, feet, and tongue in cold water with a heaping tablespoon of salt and a tablespoon of whole peppercorns or a small red pepper; boil them over the fire until the bones can be pulled out easily.

▦ Strain the broth in which the head is boiled and save for soup.

▦ Take the tongue up as soon as it is tender, strip the skin off, wrap the tongue in a wet cloth, and keep it in a cool place until it is wanted.

▦ Lay the brain for an hour in cold water containing a handful of salt. Then pull off all the outer membrane from between the folds of the brain, being careful not to break the substance. When the brain is quite freed from the membrane, put it over the fire in enough cold water to cover it with a teaspoon each of salt and whole pepper-corns; let it boil for 10 or 15 minutes; then cool it, wrap it in a wet cloth, and keep it in a cool place. The brain may be heated in any good sauce and served as a separate dish. It may also be made into fritters or croquettes, or into forcemeat balls for garnishing the calf's head by mixing it with an equal quantity of breadcrumbs, two raw eggs, and salt and pepper, and then either frying or poaching.

▦ Wash well in plenty of cold salted water the tripe—the walls and fatty portions of the stomachs of calves and cows, which is nutritious and digestible, as well as cheap. It should be boiled until tender in salted boiling water and then scraped with the back of a knife; after that, it can be pickled in scalding hot spiced vinegar or kept in milk or buttermilk for several days. In the country, it may sometimes be necessary for the housewife to understand the entire process of preparing tripe for cooking by cleaning it with either lime water or with lye made from wood ashes. Tripe is usually broiled or fried, sometimes being first breaded or rolled in flour. It is an excellent winter food, when some of the meats most generally used are scarce and expensive. If prepared for the table after the first boiling, it requires rather high seasoning.

Pork

SELECT YOUNG PIGS FOR ROASTING. A roasting pig is in prime condition when it is three to six weeks old. A good roasting pig has a soft, clean, pinkish white skin, plump hams, a short curly tail, thin delicate ears, and a soft fringe-like margin all around the tongue. As soon as it is killed, plunge it into cold water for five minutes; then rub it all over with powdered resin and put it into scalding water for one minute. Lay it on a clean board and pull and scrape off the bristles, taking care not to injure the skin. When all the bristles are removed, wash the pig thoroughly, first in warm water and then several times in plenty of cold water. Then slit the pig from the throat downward and take out the entrails, laying the heart, liver, lights, and spleen in cold salted water. Wash the pig again in cold water and wrap it from the air with a cloth wet in cold water until it is wanted for use.

BUTCHER THE HOG PROPERLY. After being properly dressed, hogs should hang long enough to get rid of the animal heat. When they are ready to be cut up, they should be divided into nine principal parts: two hams, two shoulders, two middlings, the head or face, the jowl, and the chine. The hog is laid on its back to be cut up. The head is cut off just below the ears, then it is split down each side of the backbone, which is the chine. This is divided into three pieces, the upper portion being a choice piece to be eaten cold. This fat portion may be cut off to make lard. Each half should then have the loaf fat taken out by cutting the thin skin between it and the ribs. Just under this, the next thing to be removed is the mousepiece or tenderloin, commencing at the point of the ham. This is considered the most delicate part and is used to make the nicest sausage. Just under this tenderloin are some short ribs about three inches long, running up from the point of the ham. This portion is removed by a sharp knife being run under it, taking care to cut it smooth and not too thick. When broiled, it is as nice as a partridge. The ribs are next taken out of the shoulder and middling, though some persons prefer leaving them in the middling; in this case, seven should be taken from the shoulder to make a delicious broil. Then cut off the ham as near the bone as possible, in a half circle. The shoulder is then cut square across. The feet are then chopped off with a sharp axe or cleaver. From the shoulder, the feet should be cut off leaving a stump of about two inches; from the ham, they should be cut off at the joint as smoothly as possible.

SALT THE HAMS. In order to impart redness to the hams, rub on each a teaspoon of pulverized saltpeter before salting. If the weather is very cold, warm the salt before applying it. First rub and salt the skin side well and then the fleshy side, using for the purpose a shoe sole or leather glove. No more salt should be used than a sufficiency to preserve the meat, as an excess hardens the meat. A bushel of salt is sufficient for a thousand pounds of meat. For the chine and ribs a very light sprinkling of salt will suffice.

PACK AND LEAVE THE SALTED MEAT. The meat as salted should be packed with the skin side down, where it should remain from four to six weeks according to the weather. If the weather is mild, four weeks will answer. Should the weather be very cold and the pork in an exposed place, it will freeze; and the salt, failing to penetrate the meat, will be apt to injure it. After it has taken salt sufficiently, it should be hung up for smoking.

Game Birds

STUFF AND ROAST. For partridges, pheasants, quails, or grouse, carefully cut out all the shot; wash thoroughly but quickly, using soda in the water; rinse again and dry with a clean cloth. Stuff them and sew them up. Skewer the legs and wings to the body, larder the breast with very thin slices of fat salt pork, place them in the oven, and baste with butter and water before taking up, having seasoned them with salt and pepper; or you can leave out the pork and use only butter, or cook them without stuffing. Make a gravy of the drippings thickened with browned flour. Boil up and serve in a boat.

Small birds barded and roasted

BROIL AND SERVE WITH GRAVY. These are all very fine broiled, first splitting down the back, placing on the gridiron the inside down. Cover with a baking tin and broil slowly at first. Serve with cream gravy.

Terrapin and Green Turtle

Terrapin and green turtle are distinctive enough to be made a separate course at dinner. Only the flesh, eggs, and liver of terrapin are ordinarily used. Madeira is the proper wine for terrapin, and punch is served with green turtle.

DRESS IT PROPERLY. Loosen the sides of the shells of boiled terrapin as soon as they are cool enough to handle; lift off the top shell; pull or cut apart the small bands of flesh which hold it to the spine of the terrapin; then rein the under shell. The entrails of the terrapin have the eggs and liver embedded in them, and the legs are attached to them by crossing bands of flesh. Pull off the legs, leaving the flesh attached to them; break off the sharp claws at the extremities of the feet; separate and throw away the head and put the legs on a dish. Carefully remove the eggs and put them into a bowl of hot water; separate the liver from the entrails and cut out that part of the liver which contains the small dark green gall-bag that can be seen at one side of the liver. The utmost care should be taken to avoid cutting or breaking the gall-bag; in removing it, the liver should be held over an empty dish; if the gall-bag is cut or broken, the liver should be thrown away and the hands washed before the dressing of the terrapin is resumed. Cut the liver into half-inch squares and put it with the flesh of the terrapin.

Shellfish

The custom generally prevails in this country of beginning every dinner, where there is any attempt at formality, with small shellfish served on the half-shell. Even in the inland towns of Ohio, oysters and hard clams can usually be procured, for they are now shipped in barrels from the eastern seaboard to all parts of the country accessible by rail. The proper accompaniments for raw shellfish are lemon and brown bread and butter, both of which are placed upon the table when it is laid.

HEED THIS ADVICE FOR PREPARING OYSTERS, MUSSELS, AND LOBSTERS:

☞ The newest fashion in serving raw oysters is to surround them with what is called sea moss, made by spinach, which hides the fine chopped ice in which the oysters are imbedded.

☞ If the shells of mussels are at all muddy or sandy, they should be laid for an hour or longer in a tub of cold water containing a handful of salt and then thoroughly washed before they are boiled. Place mussels in a large kettle to boil with half a pint of water and set them over the fire until the shells open; the liquor which flows from them should be carefully strained and kept to use with them. Next, take them from the shells, carefully remove all the fine filaments attached, cut off the tip of the tongue and the dark, fringe-like edge or "beard" which surrounds the gills. The thread-like filaments or moss that attach the mussel to the rocks or wharves where it is found are supposed to be more or less poisonous and should be carefully removed after boiling and before dressing. Some cooks use a silver spoon in preparing mussels, thinking that it will become blackened if they are unfit for food.

☞ Have over the fire a large pot full of boiling water, containing a handful of salt; plunge a live lobster heavy in proportion to its size head first into the boiling water, which will kill it at once, and boil it steadily for 20 minutes or until the shell turns red. As soon as it can be handled, break off the claws and tail and carefully remove the soft fins which lie close to the body where the legs join it. An ordinary iron can opener is very useful in breaking apart the shell of the lobster. After the shell is separated so that the flesh can be reached, save all the green fat, coral, and white curd-like substance which lies close to the shell; remove all flesh from the claws and body and cut it in half-inch pieces; split the shell of the tail; remove and throw away the intestine which runs through the center of the tail; and save the flesh. The lobster will then be ready to dress for recipes.

Fish

Fish is a very healthful and digestible food. Though not nearly so nutritious as meat, it is considered by many physicians a good brain food, especially if it is broiled.

CLEAN AT HOME. Although they should be cleaned at the market, one should not trust entirely to such cleaning, but pass the edge of the knife over the fish to remove any remaining scales. Wash it inside and out with a wet cloth and dry carefully with a towel. Rub it next with salt and pepper and lay it on a dish or hang it up till you are ready to cook. Never keep it lying in water, either in preparing it for cooking or in trying to keep it till the next day

Cook Fish one of These Four Ways:

❋ *Boil.* Before boiling, rub fish carefully with a little vinegar. Boil in salted boiling water, in which put one tablespoon of vinegar, allowing ten minutes to a pound. Try with a sharp-pointed needle; if it runs through easily it is done. It will require an hour to boil a large fish and about 20 minutes for a small one.

❋ *Fry.* Be careful to have boiling-hot lard in the frying pan when you go to fry fish. First rub salt and pepper and flour or meal on the fish, then keep it well covered while frying until it reaches a pretty amber color.

❋ *Broil.* Fish which are either watery or very oily are best when cooked with direct exposure to the fire. Before broiling, rub with pepper and salt and then grease with fresh butter. Lay the fish on a gridiron well greased with sweet lard and lay the tin sheet over it. When you wish to turn, take the gridiron from the fire, holding the tin sheet on top of the fish; hold them together, lay them on a table with the tin sheet down and the gridiron uppermost, raise the gridiron, and easily slide the fish onto it to put it again on the fire and

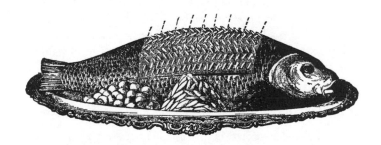

Fish larded and baked

brown the other side, putting the tin sheet back on top of it. When done, lay it on a dish and pour sauce over it.

⊛ *Bake.* Gash fish for baking straight across, half an inch deep, two inches long, and one inch apart, and then lay in strips of pork. Place in pan and cover the bottom with water half an inch deep; add one teaspoon of butter and one tablespoon of salt. Dredge fish with flour and baste often. Keep up your supply of gravy as it boils away. Try with a knitting-needle and take up with a cake turner. To lard fish for baking, remove a large piece of the skin from the back of the fish and insert lardoon. The lardoons are protected by buttered paper until the fish is nearly done; then the paper is removed to permit them to brown.

PREPARE SAUCES FOR DRY FISH. The very dry-fleshed fish should be served with a sauce. Whitefish have far less oil distributed through their bodies, are therefore not so rich as the darker-colored fish, and need richer sauces and dressings. In making sauces for fish, never use the water in which the fish has been boiled. Larded fish is generally stuffed and served with a brown mushroom sauce.

HEED THIS RECIPE FOR SAUCES. Stir pepper, salt, and minced parsley into melted butter. Or cut up one hard-boiled egg in sauce-tureen; mix half a cup of butter, half a tablespoon of flour, and one tablespoon of salt to a cream and moisten with hot water; add this to half a cup of boiling water in saucepan over fire. Let it cook till it thickens smoothly. When ready to serve, pour it over the chopped egg, stir together, and add small bits of parsley. If devilled fish is desired, add to this dressing one tablespoon pepper vinegar, one of celery vinegar, one of walnut catsup, one of made mustard, and one wineglass of acid fruit jelly.

Vegetables

Every food that has grown in the ground is called a vegetable. Not until they are growing near where we live can we expect to find them cheap. During the summer, if you can get them fresh and cook them nicely, you will not need to buy nearly as much meat and can make many nice dishes, mostly all vegetables.

BOIL OR DRY CORN. Cold boiled corn, cut from the ear and mixed with an equal quantity of cold potatoes chopped, can be fried with salt, pepper, and butter or heated with cold stewed tomatoes and served on toast. Or, cut the grains from ears of tender corn, spread them on large sheets of paper in the sun, and dry them thoroughly; or put them on pans in a cool oven and dry them. After the corn is dried, keep it in a cool, dry place. When it is wanted for the table, soak it overnight in enough water or milk to cover it; the next day boil it tender in the same water; season it with salt, pepper, and butter; and serve it hot.

PICK AND SOAK ROOTS. Roots, including carrots, oyster-plants, beets, potatoes, and parsnips, are mostly vegetables that will last all winter if properly taken care of. Toward spring you must pick off the sprouts, lest they become rank; soak them to plump them and cook them with greater care. The roots are particularly nice when they first come, if quite ripe. When young and tender they require less time to cook.

MASH POTATOES WITH SCALDING MILK; FRY IN HOT OIL. Mashed potatoes will be hard and sticky and heavy if you turn cold milk upon them while they are steaming hot; but, by adding scalding milk and beating them thoroughly, they will be light and feathery. Until served, they should be covered close with a napkin. Fried potatoes will be soaked and leathery if the fat is not hot enough and if they are not well drained when taken out.

USE SALT FOR SOME, SUGAR FOR OTHERS. Asparagus and celery are both cooked as a vegetable and seasoned with butter and salt, but rhubarb, which is more for a sauce, has only sugar cooked in it.

PRESERVE TOMATOES FOR WINTER. Take the tomatoes, when perfectly ripe and scald them in hot water in order to take off the skin easily. When skinned, boil them well in a little sugar or salt but no water. Then spread them in cakes about an inch thick and place the cakes in the sun. They will, in three or four days, be sufficiently dried to pack away in bags, which should hang in a dry place.

MAKE ITALIAN TOMATO PASTE THUS. Take a peck of tomatoes; break them and put them to boil with celery, four carrots, two onions, three tablespoons of salt, six whole peppers, six cloves, and a stick of cinnamon; let them boil together, stirring, until well done and in a fit state to pass through a sieve; then boil the pulp until it becomes thick, skimming all the time. Spread the jelly upon large plates or dishes, about half an inch thick; let it dry in the sun or oven. When quite dry, detach it from the dishes or plates, place it upon sheets of paper, and roll them up. In using the paste, dissolve it first in a little water or broth. Three inches square of the paste is enough to flavor two quarts of soup.

Macaroni and Spaghetti

Good Italian macaroni, both large and small, can now be bought in nearly all American cities.

PREPARE PROPERLY. Macaroni should never be washed before boiling; if it is dusty, wipe it with a dry cloth; put it over the fire in plenty of salted boiling water and boil it fast for ten minutes or until it is just tender; then drain it and throw it into cold water; this washing will remove the excess of farinaceous matter that makes it sticky; after cooling in the cold water, it can be heated in any sauce preferred, and the kind of sauce used will give the name to the dish; tomato, mushroom, and white sauces are usually employed.

ADD MEAT TO THE DISH. The addition of a little chopped cold ham, tongue, or chicken to macaroni makes a delicious dish; as does the addition of white and tomato sauce and some chopped mushrooms and meat or poultry. Fried onions are very good with macaroni, making the favorite Italian farmer's dish.

ADD CHEESE AND BAKE. Boiled macaroni layered with grated cheese and moistened with white sauce or a little milk and butter makes a good baked dish; a few bread crumbs may be put over the top.

Seasonings

A man is able to work longer and better if his meals are nourishing. He does not know when to add salt or pepper, and why should he? It should be the care of the wife or daughter to so season the food that the first mouthful is appetizing.

PREPARE A BOUQUET OF HERBS FOR FLAVOR. Hold a small bunch of parsley in the palm of the left hand; lay on it a small stalk of celery, a bay leaf, a sprig of any sweet herb except sage, a blade of mace, and a dozen peppercorns or a small red-pepper pod; fold the parsley so as to enclose all the other seasonings and tie it in a compact little bundle; this is called a bouquet, or fagot, of herbs, in French cookbooks, and it serves to give an indescribable and delicious flavor to the dishes in which it is cooked.

For cooking and flavoring purposes no spices are so good as the Neptune Spices, of double strength and flavor, prepared only by John H. Gause & Co., Lake Shore Coffee and Spice Mills, Cleveland, Ohio.

—Advertisement in the
Centennial Buckeye Cook Book, 1876

Relishes

The innumerable small appetizers known as relishes, or hors d'œuvres, include all forms of pickles and table sauces, small sandwiches and crusts garnished with highly seasoned meats, various preparations of cheese and eggs; in short, any small, highly spiced or seasoned dish calculated to rouse or stimulate the appetite.

Consider these Relishes:

※ *Smoked fish.* Small strips of cured fish, either salted or smoked, are acceptable as a relish; or small fish which have been preserved in oil, such as anchovies or sardines, may be wiped dry with a towel and served with vinegar or lemon juice. Smoked eels, herring, halibut, sturgeon, tunny-fish, salt codfish, salmon, Finnan haddie, Yarmouth bloaters, or any dried fish may be served; only it must be delicately prepared in small pieces and with some suitable garnish, so as to be an appreciable incentive to the enjoyment of the heavier dishes which succeed it. Sliced lemon is always a good garnish for any highly seasoned relish.

※ *Sandwich butter.* Mix together equal parts of good butter and grated ham or tongue; season rather highly with salt, cayenne, and mustard mixed with vinegar. Pack the mixture into little earthen jars; cover each jar with a piece of paper dipped in brandy and then exclude the air by a tight cover or a bladder wet and then tied over the top; keep in a cool, dry place. The flavor may be changed by varying the ingredients and seasoning.

※ *Sandwiches.* Acceptable sandwiches can be made with potted and devilled meats now sold in jars and tins. The bread should be quite free from crust, cut in thin small slices, and thinly spread with the best butter; a thin layer of seasoned meat, game, poultry, or some kind of spiced or salted fish is put between two slices of the buttered bread; irregular edges are trimmed off and the sandwiches kept cool until served. Meat or fish for sandwiches should be chopped or grated.

Relishes: Bouchées and Rissoles

❀ *Canapes.* Canapes are small slices of bread slightly hollowed out on the upper surface and then fried golden brown in plenty of smoking hot fat. The little hollow is filled with any highly seasoned meat and the canapes served either hot or cold.

❀ *Puff-Pastes.* Puff-pastes are forms of pastry made both in sweets and with delicate force-meats and ragouts to be served as hot entrees. Timbales are small patties baked in deep, smooth molds. Bouchees are very small shells of puff-paste filled with any highly seasoned mince or ragout and served both hot and cold. Rissoles, the smallest puff-paste, are turnovers filled with highly seasoned mince and either baked or fried like croquettes.

CONSIDER PICKLES AS RELISHES AND HEED THESE PICKLING TIMES:

❧ Pickle vinegar ought to be prepared several months before using and always kept on hand ready for use.

❧ Oysters must stand two days covered in stewed juice and vinegar to become pickled.

❧ Three weeks is long enough for green pickles to remain in brine, if you wish to make your pickle early in the fall.

❧ Yellow pickle must stand for two 24-hour periods in brine, poured over while hot; on the third day spread them on a board or table and let them stand in the hot sun four days, taking care that no dew shall fall on them.

❧ For boiled cucumber pickle, take fresh cucumbers, put them in brine for a few days; take them out, and put them in vinegar to soak for two days.

❧ Sweet tomato pickle will be ready for use in a fortnight after being prepared, poured into a stone jar, and sealed tight.

❧ Mangoes must have been in brine two weeks and greened, as you would cucumbers, before being stuffed and covered with vinegar in a jar to be stored.

❧ For peach mangoes, pour on syrup for three mornings, boil on the fourth, and wait a few weeks.

- Pepper mangoes must be packed closely in a stone jar (with the small end downward) in vinegar for three weeks to be ready for use.
- For chow-chow, pack ingredients in salt for a night, soak in vinegar and water for two days, boil for three mornings.

Make a Sealing Wax for Pickle Jars. Put three ounces of yellow beeswax into a small tin pail with six ounces of powdered rosin; set the pail in a pan of hot water and stir the wax and rosin until they are melted and smoothly blended. While the wax is still liquid from the action of heat, apply it to the jars or bottles containing pickles or preserves after they are corked.

Desserts

Select Desserts by the Dinner. When you have a hearty, salt-meat dinner, use a cold, light, delicate pudding, like a boiled custard. When you have a fish dinner, which does not give the nourishment that meat does, serve a boiled, hearty pudding. A lemon cornstarch pudding can be used when you are short of milk, and a broken cold pudding can be made fresh again by arranging it in a clean dish and covering it with a meringue.

Take Care to Heat the Oven Properly for Cakes. A layer of sand on the bottom of the oven, about half an inch thick, is a safeguard against burning on the bottom. If the general heat is too great, the cake will burn or crack on the top before it can bake properly; if the oven is not hot enough, the cake will not rise properly. A very safe test of the heat is to put a spoonful of the cake dough or batter on a bit of buttered paper and slip it into the oven; this may be done during the final mixing of the cake so that it will not have to stand after it is ready for the oven; if the little cake bakes evenly and quickly without burning at the edge, the heat is right and the large cake may be put into the oven.

BAKE DEEP CAKES WITH PAPER. When a cake pan is too shallow for the quantity of cake desired, extend it with stiff glazed paper thickly coated with butter; if the oven heat is moderate, the butter will preserve the paper from burning.

HAVE LIGHTNESS IN MIND WHEN BAKING. Whoever eats heavy pie crust commits a crime against his physical well being. The good house-wife should see to it that all pastry and cakes are light.

USE A FREEZER TO MAKE ICE CREAM. The secret of making good ice cream lies in the freezing. The old way of freezing cream, which is still in use among small confectioners, consisted of occasionally stirring the cream while it was freezing in a tin can set in a tub of ice and salt. A more easy and expeditious method is within the reach of the average housekeeper in these days of patent freezers. The principle underlying all the best-known patents is the mixing of the cream by a wooden beater which revolves inside the can by the same motion that slightly changes the position of the can in the outer tub of ice and salt.

TAKE CARE IN PREPARING THE ICE-CREAM MIXTURE. Ice creams of the most ordinary sort are made of milk thickened with arrowroot or cornstarch in the proportion of a tablespoon to a quart, dissolved in cold water, and boiled in milk, which is cooled, sweetened, and flavored before frozen. The freezing mixture should be composed of three parts of crushed ice to one of coarse salt, and care should be taken that it does not reach high enough around the sides of the can to penetrate to the interior and so spoil the cream; the water formed in the outer tub by the melting of the freezing mixture is intensely cold and need not be drawn off while the cream is being frozen unless it is likely to get into the can.

COLOR THE CREAM IF YOU WISH. Boil very slowly in a gill of water, till reduced to half, 20 grains of cochineal and the same of alum and of finely powdered cream of tartar; strain and keep in a phial, tightly corked. For yellow coloring use an infusion of saffron; for green, use spinach leaves boiled and the juice expressed; for red, express the juice from the pokeberry. To every pint allow a pound of sugar and boil 15 minutes. A teaspoon of this jelly will color two quarts of milk.

Spirits

ENLIVEN ORDINARY DISHES WITH THE ADDITION OF SPIRITS:

- A little brandy will improve calf's head soup, though it is a delightful soup as it is.
- Just before dinner add a glass of claret or Madeira wine to turtle soup.
- Add brandy and wine to mock turtle soup.
- When rump or beef stew is served up, pour a little wine over it and strew the top with all-spice.
- Half an hour before dishing up beef tongue stew, add one-half wineglass of wine and seasonings and stew awhile together.
- When the water has nearly stewed away from rabbit stew, add half a pint of Port wine and let it stew gently till quite tender.
- Put a little white wine in the pan with seasoned half-roasted pigeons, a quart of good gravy, and additional seasonings.
- Just before dishing up calves' feet dressed as terrapins, add two wineglasses of good cooking wine and simmer again before serving.
- Add a glass of wine just before taking up tongue à la terrapin.
- Just before dinner, put a glass of red wine in haunch of venison and let it stew a little longer.
- As you remove turtles from the fire, pour in one-half pint Madeira wine.
- When fish salad is cold put over it a little Worcestershire sauce and sherry wine.
- Season tartaric cakes with mace or wine.
- When ready to boil English plum pudding, wet all the ingredients with ten eggs, well beaten, two wineglasses of wine, and the same of brandy.
- Serve sippet pudding hot with a rich sauce made of sugar and butter seasoned with nutmeg and Madeira wine.

- Add one winglass of wine to recipe for orange pie.
- The requisite quantity of pale Madeira or sherry should be added to jelly, baked custard, creams, and Charlotte Russe after the other ingredients have been well boiled together.
- For frozen pudding, put in the wine when syrup is nearly boiling; add last a wineglass of brandy.
- If you like, pour good Madeira or sherry wine over ambrosia.
- Mix into ingredients for pancakes four tablespoons Madeira wine.
- Add brandy to crab cider, so much as you think best.

CHAPTER FOUR

DAILY AND SEASONAL COOKING TASKS

Daily Tasks

Every moment has its appointed duty, and one neglected never comes back to give us a new trial.

AT SUNRISE:

- 🕸 Kill the turtle in summer for turtle soup and hang it up to bleed.
- 🕸 Sift flour for plum pudding; in winter, set it in a warm place, in summer set it in a cool pace to rise.

BEFORE BREAKFAST:

- 🕸 Always shape and put bread in the molds.
- 🕸 Always try to make cake before breakfast or as early in the morning as possible.
- 🕸 Before breakfast, begin preparing vegetable soup for dinner, if served at two o'clock.

IN THE COOL OF THE MORNING:

- 🕸 Try to churn, as fewer flies are swarming then, and the butter can be made much firmer.
- 🕸 Also, print butter, make pastry, and gather vegetables.

- ❦ If you are living in the city, get your vegetables from market as early in the morning as possible.

AFTER BREAKFAST:

- ❦ Make leaven in winter.
- ❦ Set dough to rise at eleven o'clock in the morning for early tea.
- ❦ Blanch Jordan almonds that have been soaked overnight for cheesecakes, using cold water; lay them on a clean cloth to dry, and then beat them fine in a marble mortar with a little orange-flower or rose water.
- ❦ In cool weather, make fritters about nine o' clock in the morning; in summer, about eleven o' clock.
- ❦ It is well to make ice cream early in the day and set it aside, leaving more leisure for other preparations that are better made immediately before dinner.
- ❦ Begin preparing stewed chicken for dinner immediately after breakfast.
- ❦ Begin cooking corned beef tongue for dinner; put the beef on in a large pot of water early in the morning and simmer for hours.
- ❦ Make up yeast in the morning; it ought to be fit for use at night.
- ❦ Sun and air flour, whether old or new, before using; in the morning, get out the flour to be made up at night for next morning's breakfast, sift it in a tray, and put it out in the sun; or, if the day is damp, set it near the kitchen fire.

IN THE EVENING:

- ❦ Send the children to gather up vegetables, as well as cut flowers, to garnish cold meats and salads for the next day's dinner.
- ❦ Pick fully ripe figs for fig preserves the evening before and let them soak all night in very weak salt water.
- ❦ Set dried peas to soak overnight, hominy in hot water to boil the next day; salt pork in skimmed milk to bake like fresh pork for salt pork almost as good as fresh roast pork; ingredients for liver pudding (hog's heads, livers, milts, sweetbreads, kidneys) together in a

tub of salt and water; Jordan almonds in cold water for almond cheesecake; tapioca in a little water for tapioca cream.

❀ Prepare the fruit for fruit cake the day before.

❀ Kill the chicken the day before broiling.

Seasonal Tasks

In Summer:

❀ In May, make pickle vinegar, which should sun all summer.

❀ Kill and dress the poultry the day beforehand, except chicken for frying, which is not good unless killed the same day it is eaten.

❀ Make bread dough with cold water; apply no artificial heat to it, but set it in a cool place to ferment.

In Fall:

❀ Bottle currant wine in September.

❀ Late as possible in the fall prepare tender roasting ears for winter use.

❀ In cool weather, set dough before the fire, both before and after making it into rolls.

❀ In October and November, engage butter to be brought weekly, fresh from the churn in rolls.

In Winter:

❀ Corned beef prepared in January will keep well through the month of March, improving with the lapse of time.

❀ Put beef and tongue, about the middle of February, in brine; rub first with salt and let them lie for a fortnight, then throw them in brine and let them lie there three weeks before hanging in a cool, dark place.

❀ A smothered fire for curing bacon should be made up three times a day till the middle of March or first of April.

❀ Make bread dough with lukewarm water in winter; make it up at seven o' clock in the evening, and then set it on a shelf under which a lighted coal-oil lamp is placed. Set yeast in a warm place in the winter to ferment.

🏵 It is well to keep soup stock on hand in cold weather, as by the addition of a can of tomatoes, or other ingredients, a delicious soup may be quickly made of it.

IN SPRING:

🏵 Draw off crab cider in March, and it is fit for use.

🏵 In curing bacon, the joint pieces should be taken down in the middle of March or first of April and packed in hickory or other green-wood ashes, as in salt, where they will remain all the summer without danger of bugs interfering with them.

🏵 In curing hams, on the first of April, take them down and pack in any coal ashes or pine ashes well slaked.

🏵 It is best to scald the vinegar in the spring when making oil mangoes.

🏵 The liquid for yellow pickle vinegar should be spiced in the spring and set in the sun until autumn.

PART FIVE

Recipes

BREADS

Breakfast Corn Cake

Some years ago business called me to pass through Toledo several times, and I stayed overnight, each time, at the Island House, where I found so much better corn bread at the breakfast table than I had ever eaten. According to my custom when traveling and finding some dish extra nice, I obtained the recipe, through influence of the waiter girl, as "mail carrier" (paying a price equal to the price of this book) who wrote it out for me in my diary while I ate my breakfast. I think I have eaten of it more than 100 times since, but I have never seen corn cake to excel it. Here it is:

  1 quart corn meal
  1 cup flour, or a little less
  1 tablespoon baking powder
  milk, to wet
  1 or 2 eggs
  sugar and salt to taste

Combine first 4 ingredients. Beat in 1 or 2 eggs and add a little sugar and salt. Put into a dripping pan and put at once into a hot oven, but do not dry it up by overbaking. It should be 1 to 1½ inches thick when baked.

—*Dr. Chase's Third Last and Complete Receipt Book and Household Physician (Memorial Edition)*, 1903

Maple Rolls

  1 ½ cups flour
  1 ½ teaspoons Rumford Baking Powder
  ⅓ teaspoon salt
  2 tablespoons butter
  about ¾ cup milk
  scraped maple sugar

Sift together the flour, baking powder, and salt; rub in the butter as lightly as possible with the fingers, just working it until the fat is well blended with the flour. When well mixed, add the milk, using enough to make a soft dough. Roll this out on a floured board, about one-third inch thick, spread thickly with the scraped maple sugar, roll up like a jelly roll, and cut into slices with a very sharp knife. Lay these on a greased baking pan and bake from 12 to 15 minutes.
—*Rumford Complete Cook Book,* 1908

Excellent Light Biscuits

  4 large Irish potatoes
  lard the size of an egg
  1 teacup milk
  1 teacup yeast
  about 2 quarts flour

Boil potatoes. While hot, mash them with the lard. Add the milk and yeast. Stir in flour to make a good batter and set it to rise. When light, make up the dough. You generally have to add more water or milk. Roll thick and let them rise slowly, but bake them quickly.
—*Practical American Cookery,* 1885

Old-Fashioned Indian or Corn Bread

This recipe which I have is the nearest to the old Dutch-oven corn bread of anything that can now be baked.

2 pint cups of Indian meal
1 pint cup of flour
2 pint cups of sweet milk
1 pint cup of sour milk
½ pint cup of sugar
1 teaspoon salt
1 teaspoon soda

Mix ingredients and bake for 1½ hours.

—Mrs. S. N. Ross, Sparta, Ohio
Dr. Chase's Third Last and Complete Receipt Book and
Household Physician (Memorial Edition), 1903

Quick Breakfast Puffs

2 eggs
1 cup milk
1 tablespoon melted butter
1 ½ cups flour
2 teaspoons Rumford Baking Powder
½ teaspoon salt

Beat the eggs very thoroughly and add the milk and butter. Sift the flour, salt, and baking powder twice; add the liquid ingredients and beat 2 minutes. Pour into hot, well-greased muffin pans and bake 20 minutes in a hot oven.

—*Rumford Complete Cook Book*, 1908

Recipes for Stale Bread

MILK TOAST. Milk Toast, to be nice, must be crisp, brown, and tender but not so soft that the cream will soak into it; care should be taken that the milk be in readiness when the toast is made, so that the toast will not have time to steam before the milk is poured over it. The cream dressing should not be quite so thick as condensed milk but a little thicker than common cream. Cornstarch or flour may be used as thickening devices.

WELSH RARE-BIT. The only difference between Milk Toast and Welsh Rare-bit is in the dressing, which for the latter contains a little grated cheese and an egg. Gentlemen usually enjoy Welsh Rare-bit, which can be a very inviting dish for supper.

STALE BREAD BATTER CAKES. Put a loaf of stale bread to stand all day in a pint of milk. Just before tea add 3 eggs and 1 large spoon of butter. If too thin, add a little flour.

BREADING. Stale bread may be laid aside until thoroughly dried, then rolled very fine. Put this into a wide-mouthed bottle into which you can dip a spoon. This is useful in many ways, as in breading veal chops or oysters.

QUEEN TOAST. Queen toast is made by soaking the slices in a very plain uncooked custard and browning in a frying pan. When served, sugar and cinnamon are sprinkled between the slices as they are piled upon the dish.

TOAST CRUMBS. Toast crumbs are made of buttered bread cut in very small cubes and placed in the oven to brown. These are very nice served with soup, and it is a good way to use up very small pieces of bread.

Fritters, Plain and Quick

I call these Johnny Jumpup Cakes, because they jump up from the bottom of the hot lard so quickly and lightly.

4 eggs
1 pint sweet milk
1 teaspoon salt
1 tablespoon baking powder
2 or 3 cups flour

Beat the eggs well, stir in milk and salt; then put the baking powder into the flour and stir in, using as much flour as will stir in well; drop into hot lard. Eat with maple syrup or syrup made by dissolving granulated sugar.

—"Ivy," West Jefferson, Ohio
Dr. Chase's Third Last and Complete Receipt Book and
Household Physician (Memorial Edition), 1903

Wheat-Flour Griddle Cakes

1 pint milk
3 eggs
4 tablespoons melted butter
1 ½ cups flour
1 ½ teaspoons baking powder

Mix milk with eggs, the yolks and whites beaten separately. Add melted butter. Sift flour with baking powder and add to the above. Bake on a hot griddle.

—*Mrs. Seely's Cook Book,* 1902

EGGS, OMELETS,
AND CHEESE

Poached Eggs

Have salted boiling water in the frying pan. Drop each egg in separately. When the white is set, baste. With a skimmer remove each egg and serve on buttered toast.

—*Cooking Garden*, 1885

Eggs in Cases

Make little paper cases of buttered writing paper; put a small piece of butter and a little chopped parsley or onion in each; pepper and salt. Place the cases upon a gridiron over a moderate fire of bright coals.

When the butter melts, break a fresh egg into each case. Strew in upon them a few seasoned breadcrumbs, and when nearly done, glaze the tops with a hot shovel. Serve in the paper cases.

—*The White House Cook Book*, 1887

Tomatoes and Eggs

3 or 4 firm, round tomatoes
2 eggs
1 teaspoon butter
1 wineglass cream
a little onion juice
1 tablespoon grated Parmesan cheese
pinches of salt, pepper, and sugar

Cut tomatoes in half and place them in a fire-proof baking dish, skin down. Add 1 tablespoon of water and bake until tender. Remove from oven before they lose their shape and scoop out a good portion from each. Break eggs into a saucepan and add butter, cream, onion juice, Parmesan cheese, salt, pepper, and sugar. Whisk all until thick and creamy. Fill tomato cups with custard and decorate with a sprig of parsley. Serve very hot on toast.
—*High Living*, 1904

Vegetable Omelet

vegetables such as cucumbers, artichokes, onions, sorrel, green peas, tomatoes, lentils, mushrooms, asparagus tops, potatoes, truffles, or turnips
milk, cream, or gravy
eggs
1 teaspoon butter

Make a puree by mashing up ready-dressed vegetables with a little milk, cream, or gravy and some seasoning. Prepare eggs by beating them very lightly. Pour them into a nice hot frying pan containing butter; spread the puree upon the upper side; when perfectly hot, turn or fold the omelet together and serve. Or cold vegetables may be merely chopped small, then tossed in a little butter, and some beaten and seasoned eggs poured over them.
—*The White House Cook Book*, 1887

Premium Cheese.

For a cheese of 20 pounds, a piece of rennet about 2 inches square is soaked about 12 hours in 1 pint of water. As rennets differ much in quality, enough should be used to coagulate the milk sufficiently in about 40 minutes. No salt is put into the cheese, nor any outside during the first 6 or 8 hours it is being prepared, but a thin coat of fine Liverpool salt is kept on the outside during the remainder of the time it remains in press. Tile cheeses are pressed 48 hours under a weight of 7 or 8 cwt. Nothing more is required but to turn the cheeses once a day on the shelves.

—*Wright's Book of 3000 Practical Receipts*, 1869

SOUPS

Ox-Tail Soup

> ox-tail
> flour
> salt and pepper
> 2 tablespoons butter
> 1 carrot
> 1 turnip
> 1 onion
> 1 tablespoon any good table sauce

Cut an ox-tail in pieces about an inch long, wash it well in plenty of cold water. Put it over the fire in fresh cold water enough to cover it and let it slowly reach the boiling point. Then drain and dry it, roll it in flour seasoned with salt and pepper, put it over the fire in a saucepan containing butter made smoking hot, and brown it. While the ox-tail is being browned, peel and dice the carrot, turnip, and onion. When the ox-tail is brown, add the vegetables to it, together with 3 quarts of boiling water and a palatable seasoning of salt and pepper. Boil the soup slowly for 3 hours, keeping the saucepan covered; then add table sauce and serve the soup.

—*Practical American Cookery*, 1885

Pea Soup

    1/4 pint peas
    1 small strip of salt pork
    1 teaspoon salt
    celery seed
    small piece of onion

Mix peas, 1 pint of cold water, salt pork, salt, and a little celery seed. Fry a small piece of onion till brown and add to above. Cover and boil all together 4 or 5 hours. Rub through a colander.

—*Cooking Garden*, 1885

Chestnut Soup

    1 quart large Italian chestnuts
    1 teaspoon salt
    lemon rind
    2 quarts veal or chicken broth
    1 wineglass cream
    1 tablespoon butter rolled in flour

Boil Italian chestnuts for 20 minutes. Take off the shells and thin brown skin. Put them into a saucepan with enough boiling water to cover them. Add salt and a piece of lemon rind. When soft, rub through a sieve. Then pour over them, stirring all the time, good veal or chicken broth, cream, and butter rolled in flour. Bring to a boil. Serve very hot. This will be sufficient for 8 persons.

—*High Living*, 1904

Green Turtle Soup Stock

    4 pounds turtle flesh
    veal bones or calf's head or feet
    1 tablespoon salt
    1 carrot
    1 turnip
    1 onion
    a dozen cloves
    bouquet of parsley
    sweet herbs, mace, and peppercorns

Allow a gallon of cold water for every four pounds of turtle flesh. Put over the fire together with an even weight of veal bones or calf's head or feet, salt, carrot, turnip, onion peeled and stuck with cloves, parsley, sweet herbs, mace, and peppercorns. (As fast as any portion of the turtle becomes tender, take it up, cool it, wrap it in a wet cloth, and put it in a cool place to use in recipes.) Continue to boil the bones and shells for 5 or 6 hours; then, as when juices of any meat have been extracted, the liquor should be strained into a stone jar.

SALADS

Dutch Salad

    a dozen anchovies
    1 herring
    Bologna or Lyons sausage or smoked ham and sausages
    breast of cold roast fowl or veal
    beet-roots

pickled cucumbers
potatoes
1 tablespoon capers
hard-boiled eggs
a dozen stoned olives
oil
Tarragon vinegar
white pepper
French mustard

Wash, split, and bone anchovies and roll each one up. Wash, split, and bone one herring and cut into small pieces. Dice an equal quantity of Bologna or Lyons sausage or smoked ham and sausages. Also add an equal quantity of the breast of cold roast fowl or veal. Add likewise, always in the same quantity, diced beet-roots, pickled cucumbers, and cold boiled potatoes cut in larger pieces; use at least thrice as much potato as anything else. Add capers, the yolks and whites of some hard-boiled eggs, minced separately, and stoned olives; mix all the ingredients well together, reserving the olives and anchovies to ornament the top of the bowl. Beat up together oil and Tarragon vinegar with white pepper and French mustard to taste; pour this over the salad and serve.
—*The White House Cook Book,* 1877

Hunter's Salad

Cut cold wild ducks into thin slices and marinate in French dressing for several hours in a cold place. Shred a large head of celery into long thick strips, place in a salad bowl and pile the meat in the center. Garnish with finely chopped hard-boiled eggs.
—*High Living,* 1904

Marshmallow Salad

10-cent can marshmallows
½ cup English walnut meats

½ pound white grapes, cut in halves and seeded
1 small pineapple
1 orange
salt
mayonnaise dressing
whipped cream

Cut marshmallows with scissors into 5 or 6 pieces. Add English walnut meats and white grapes. In a separate dish shred the pineapple and orange. When ready to serve arrange the latter on leaves of head lettuce that have been sprinkled with salt; cover over with the marshmallows, grapes, and nuts, and crown the top with mayonnaise dressing that has been mixed with a little whipped cream; any citrus fruit may be used.

—*Grayville Cook Book*, 1912

BEEF

Pot Roast of Beef

4 pounds top sirloin of beef
2 tablespoons flour
seasoning
diced onions, carrots, and turnips
3 tablespoons drippings or other fat

Have the meat cut in a thick, compact piece. If necessary, tie and skewer so that it will keep its shape. Melt a little fat in a saucepan (an old-fashioned, round bottom "Scotch bowl" is the best) and brown the meat on all sides; pour 1 quart boiling water over it and cover closely. Simmer as gently as possible for 2 hours; then season and add the vegetables. Cook till the vegetables are tender; then remove the meat and vegetables from the pan and thicken the gravy with the flour mixed smoothly with a little cold water. If necessary add more water while the roast is cooking that there may be sufficient gravy to cover the vegetables.

—*Rumford Complete Cook Book,* 1908

Devilled Roast Beef Bones

Take the bones from cold roast beef, leaving as much meat as possible on them. Season with salt and pepper, and rub them with mustard paste. Roll in fresh broad crumbs and sprinkle each one with little pieces of butter. Broil over a slow fire until a nice brown and serve on a hot dish and with thickened brown gravy around them, or over them, as you wish.

—*Mrs. Seely's Cook Book,* 1902

Beef Hash

To two parts cold roast or boiled corned beef, chopped fine, put one of mashed potatoes and a little pepper, salt, milk, and melted butter. Turn all into a frying pan and stir until it is heated through and smoking hot, but not until it browns. Put into a deep dish and, if stiff enough, shape as you would mashed potato, into a hillock. Or, you can cease stirring for a few minutes and let a brown crust form on the under side; then turn out whole into a flat dish, the brown side uppermost. Or, mould the mixture into flat cakes; dip these in beaten eggs and fry in hot drippings. A little catsup and mustard are an improvement to plain cold beef, thus hashed.

—*Common Sense in the Household,* 1871

Cold Beef and Dry Bread or Biscuit Balls

Cold beef may be economically "turned," as we say of re-making a dress, into a new dish, which may even have a nicer relish than in its first form or "dress."

    beef
    bread
    3 eggs
    salt to taste
    nutmeg

Chop your beef very fine (pork will not do). Then soak your bread in cold water till it is soft, then take it in the hands and squeeze as much of the water out as you can, having two-thirds as much bread as meat. Mix the bread and meat thoroughly together; beat eggs well and mix in. Add salt to taste and grate in enough nutmeg to season nicely. Make out in balls about the size of a small biscuit and fry slowly in butter or cooking fat till brown on both sides.

—"Winifred," Toledo, Ohio

Dr. Chase's Third Last and Complete Receipt Book and Household Physician (Memorial Edition), 1903

VEAL

Veal Klopps

    2 cups finely minced veal
    juice of 1 small onion
    salt and pepper to taste

a little grated lemon rind
unbeaten whites of 3 eggs

Add the onion juice, seasoning, and lemon rind to the minced veal and form a paste of the seasoned meat with the whites of the eggs. Shape with the hands into very small balls and, when all are ready, drop a few at a time into boiling salted water in a shallow pan and cook gently for five minutes. Serve on rounds of buttered toast. Cover with either a tomato sauce or rich white sauce.

—*Rumford Complete Cook Book*, 1908

MUTTON

Mutton Chops

If your butcher has not done it, and the chances are he has not, unless you stood by to see it attended to, trim off the superfluous fat and skin, so as to give the chops a certain litheness and elegance of shape. Dip each in beaten egg, roll in pounded cracker, and fry in hot lard or dripping. If the fat is unsalted, sprinkle the chops with salt before rolling in the egg. Serve up dry and hot. Or, you may omit the egg and cracker and broil on a gridiron over a bright fire. Put a little salt and pepper upon each chop and butter them before they go to the table. Cook lamb chops in the same way.

—*Common Sense in the Household*, 1871

Stuffed Shoulder of Mutton

    1 good-sized shoulder of mutton
    1 cup bread crumbs

1 tablespoon chopped parsley
grated rind of half a lemon
1 tablespoon chopped suet or drippings
salt and pepper to taste
1 egg

Remove the blade bone from the shoulder, or have the butcher do it. Put the bread crumbs into a bowl with the parsley, lemon, suet, salt, and pepper and mix them with the well-beaten egg. Stuff the cavity from which the bone was removed, sew up the opening, and roast, basting frequently with a little fat or the meat will be dry. Allow 15 minutes to the pound. Serve with a thick, brown gravy.

—*Rumford Complete Cook Book*, 1908

LAMB

Lamb Stew (with Dumplings)

3 to 4 pounds lamb
½ pound salt pork
1 onion
pepper
parsley and thyme
2 spoons flour
1 cup cold milk
green corn (optional)

Cut up lamb, the inferior portions will do as well as any other, crack the bones, and remove all the fat. Put on the meat—the pieces not more than an inch and a half in length—in a pot with enough cold

water to cover well, and set it where it will heat gradually. Add nothing else until it has stewed an hour, closely covered; then throw in the salt pork cut into strips, the chopped onion, and some pepper; cover and stew an hour longer or until the meat is very tender. Make out a little paste, as for the crust of a meat pie; cut into squares and drop in the stew. Boil ten minutes and season further by the addition of a little parsley and thyme. Thicken with flour stirred into cold milk. Boil up once and serve in a tureen or deep-covered dish. If green corn is in season, this stew is greatly improved by adding, an hour before it is taken from the fire, the grains of half a dozen ears, cut from the cob. Try it for a cheap family dinner, and you will repeat the experiment often.
—*Common Sense in the Household*, 1871

Broiled Lamb's Kidneys

    a dozen kidneys
    salt and pepper
    sweet oil
    bread crumbs
    Madeira

Skin, trim, and split lengthwise the kidneys. Put them in a dish and season with salt, pepper, and sweet oil. Then put them on skewers—if not silver, have them bright and fresh looking. Run the skewer through the center of the 2 kidneys; do not separate them. Roll in fine bread crumbs and broil over a moderate fire for 5 minutes. Serve on a folded napkin with a thick brown sauce seasoned with Madeira in a separate dish.
—*Mrs. Seely's Cook Book*, 1902

PORK

Breakfast Scrapple

Scrapple is a most palatable, cheap, and delicious breakfast dish, especially cut into slices when cold, and fried brown, as you do mush. To make it, take the head, heart, and any lean scraps of pork and boil until the flesh slips easily from the bones. Remove the fat, gristle, and bones, then chop finely. Set the liquor in which the meat was boiled aside until cold, take the cake of fat from the surface and return to the fire. When it boils, put in the chopped meat and season well with pepper and salt. Let it boil again, then thicken with cornmeal as you would in making ordinary cornmeal mush, by letting it slip through the fingers slowly to prevent lumps. Cook an hour, stirring constantly at first, afterwards putting back on the range in a position to boil gently. When done, pour into a long, square pan, not too deep, and mold. In cold weather this can be kept several weeks.

—*The White House Cook Book*, 1887

Pickled Pigs' Feet

> a dozen pigs' feet
> salt
> spiced vinegar
> 2 eggs
> 1 cup milk

1 teaspoon butter
flour

Scrape and wash pigs' feet and put them into a saucepan with enough hot (not boiling) water to cover them. When partly done, salt them. It requires 4 to 5 hours to boil them soft. Pack them in a stone crock and pour over them spiced vinegar made hot. They will be ready to use in a day or two. If you wish them for breakfast, split them, make a batter of eggs, milk, salt, and butter, with flour enough to make a thick batter; dip each piece in this and fry in hot lard. Or, dip them in beaten egg and flour and fry. Souse is good eaten cold or warm.
—*The White House Cook Book*, 1887

Curing Ham or Other Meat for Smoking, without Pickle

This recipe has been in use in my family eight years, while, if not good, one year would have been sufficient.

WARRANTED TO KEEP ALL SUMMER. Take 1 pound saltpeter, 1 pound pepper, 3 pounds brown sugar and 10 quarts salt to 1000 weight of pork. Dissolve the saltpeter in a very little hot water; mix all the ingredients well and then rub it on and into the meat—hams, etc.—with the hand, until it is everywhere covered. Insert your finger under the center bone in hams and shoulders, and then fill that opening with the mixture. Then lay in a cool place for about 2 weeks, not allowing it to freeze, when it will be ready to smoke. This recipe has been tried and tested by a number of people and is a preventive in keeping off all troublesome insects. The meat will be sweet and tender and warranted to keep all summer. If used on beef, 1 week would be long enough to lay instead of 2 for pork, as it takes salt or other seasoning quicker than pork.
—Mrs. S. Weaver, Columbiana, Ohio
   *Dr. Chase's Third Last and Complete Receipt Book and
   Household Physician (Memorial Edition)*, 1903

CHICKEN

Chicken en Casserole

   1 young chicken
   3 tablespoons butter
   1 small onion
   1 small carrot
   1 bay leaf
   a few mushrooms, canned or fresh
   2 cups stock or water
   3 potatoes
   salt and pepper to taste
   3 tablespoons sherry

Clean, singe, and cut the chicken into pieces convenient for serving. Melt the butter in a small frying pan, add the onion and carrot, both cut in thin slices, also the pieces of chicken, and cook all till golden brown, placing them in the casserole as they reach this stage. Pour the stock over them, put in the bay leaf, and cover closely. When nearly done, add the potatoes sliced, the mushrooms, and seasoning. Cover and finish the cooking. Add the sherry at the last moment before serving and send to table in the casserole.

—*Rumford Complete Cook Book*, 1908

Shaker Chicken Breast in Cider and Cream

> 4 8-ounce chicken breasts
> 5 tablespoons butter, heated
> ½ cup cider
> 1 tablespoon grated lemon rind
> 1 cup heavy cream
> 1 teaspoon each salt and pepper

Season chicken breast with salt and pepper. Saute chicken breast in hot butter until brown. Cover pan and continue cooking over low heat until tender, 15–20 minutes. Add cider and lemon rind and spoon this liquid over chicken. If chicken seems to be drying out, add cider before chicken is fully cooked to tender point. Remove chicken to warm serving platter. Quickly add cream and seasonings to frying pan and stir around to mix with pan juices. Pour this hot sauce over chicken on platter. Serves 4.

—The Golden Lamb, Ohio's Oldest Inn, Lebanon, Ohio
  Paul Resetar (Golden Lamb Manager),
  Personal Communication, July 10, 2001

GAME

Squirrel Pie

> pair of squirrels
> 1 pound beef suet
> 1 ½ pounds flour

2 level teaspoons salt

1 level teaspoon pepper

After the squirrels have been skinned, wipe them all over with a wet cloth to remove the hairs, and cut them in joints, saving the blood, and removing the entrails. The liver, heart, and kidneys may be used. Finely chop the beef suet, rejecting all the membrane; mix it with the flour, salt, and pepper. Butter an earthen baking dish; add enough cold water to the suet and flour to make a crust which can be rolled out about three-quarters of an inch thick. Line the dish with the crust, put in the squirrel meat and blood, adding enough cold water to half fill the pie; season it highly with salt and pepper, and cover with the crust, wetting all the edges to make them adhere so closely that the gravy cannot escape. In the middle of the top crust, cut a little slit, to permit the escape of the steam while the pie is being baked. Bake the pie in a moderate oven for about 2 hours; when the crust is nearly brown enough, cover it with buttered paper. When the pie is done, serve it hot in the dish in which it was baked.

—*Practical American Cookery*, 1885

Filets of Wild Duck with Orange-Sauce

breast or filets of wild duck

Seville or bitter orange

gill of broth

glass of Madeira

salt and cayenne pepper

For this dish, use only the breast or filets of wild duck, either broiled or roasted rare. While they are being cooked, cut the rind of a Seville or bitter orange in small shreds and squeeze the juice; put the orange rind and juice into a saucepan with the broth and Madeira. Season the sauce palatably with salt and cayenne. Simmer it for 5 minutes, then serve it with the filets of wild duck.

—*Practical American Cookery*, 1885

FISH

Stewed Fish

    1 large onion
    2 or 3 tablespoons olive oil
    2 pounds of any kind of whitefish
    salt and cayenne pepper
    12 eggs
    juice of 2 lemons
    1 tablespoon vinegar
    1 tablespoon chopped parsley

Slice onion and cook without browning in olive oil. When transparent, add whitefish, cut in pieces. Add salt and cayenne and cover with water. Simmer 20 to 30 minutes. Beat together the egg yolks and add the lemon juice and vinegar. Stir into this very slowly some of the hot fish broth and the chopped parsley. Pour this over the fish and simmer until the sauce thickens. Be careful not to boil it, as the sauce would curdle.

—*High Living*, 1904

Garlic Sauce for Fish

    clove of garlic
    yolk of 1 egg
    1 tablespoon bread crumbs

milk
pinches of salt and cayenne pepper
7 to 8 teaspoons olive oil
juice of 1 lemon

Grate garlic and add egg yolk; rub smooth and add bread crumbs which have been soaked in milk and squeezed dry and a pinch of salt and cayenne pepper. Stir in olive oil and the lemon juice. If it is too thick, add a little water.
—*High Living*, 1904

Parsley-Egg Sauce for Fish

minced parsley
1 hard-boiled egg
½ cup butter
½ tablespoon flour
1 teaspoon salt
pepper
cream
1 tablespoon pepper vinegar
1 tablespoon celery vinegar
1 tablespoon walnut catsup
1 tablespoon made mustard
1 wineglass of acid fruit jelly

Stir pepper, salt, and minced parsley into melted butter. Or cut up one hard-boiled egg in sauce-tureen; mix butter, flour, and salt to a cream and moisten with hot water; and add this to a half cup of boiling water in saucepan over fire. Let it cook till it thickens smoothly. When ready to serve, pour it over the chopped egg, stir together, and add small bits of parsley. If devilled fish is desired, add to this dressing pepper vinegar, celery vinegar, walnut catsup, made mustard, and acid fruit jelly.

VEGETABLES

Peppers Stuffed with Corn

    red or green bell peppers
    a dozen ears of corn
    1 tablespoon butter
    1 tablespoon thick cream
    2 eggs
    salt to taste

Parboil the bell peppers. Leave the stems on but cut a small slice from one side of each pepper. Remove the seeds and fill with the following mixture: corn, butter, thick cream, well-beaten eggs, and salt, and fill each pepper. Replace the slice previously cut out and bake in a quick oven. Summer squash cooked in the same way are delicious.
—*High Living*, 1904

Escaloped Tomatoes

    1 pint tomatoes
    ½ cup bread crumbs
    a little butter and flour
    salt and pepper

Put a layer of bread crumbs in the bottom of a baking dish and season them with salt, pepper, and butter. Then put a layer of tomatoes

dredged with flour and seasoned. Continue till the dish is full, having the crumbs on the top.
—*Cooking Garden*, 1885

Boiled Spinach

> spinach
> salt and pepper
> butter the size of an egg
> 4 eggs

Pick the spinach over very carefully; it is apt to be gritty. Wash in several waters and let it lie in the last half of an hour at least. Take out with your hands, shaking each bunch well, and put into boiling water, with a little salt. Boil from 15 to 20 minutes. When tender, drain thoroughly, chop very fine; put into a saucepan with butter, and pepper to taste. Stir until very hot, turn into a dish, and shape into a flat-topped mound with a silver or wooden spoon; slice some hard-boiled eggs and lay on top. Or, rub the yolks of the eggs to a powder, mix with butter, and when your mound is raised, spread smoothly over the flat top. Cut the whites into rings and garnish, laying them on the yellow surface. This makes a pleasant dressing for the spinach.
—*Common Sense in the Household*, 1871

Very Nice Baked Cabbage

I knew from the nicety of this dish that the cook was a wife that a farmer ought to be proud of, or, as the saying goes now, might well afford to "tie to."

> firm head of white cabbage
> salt and pepper
> 1 tablespoon butter
> 2 eggs
> 3 tablespoons rich milk or cream

Select a firm head of white cabbage, quarter, rinse, and boil 15 minutes; pour off this water and put on more hot water and continue to boil until tender; drain off the water and set aside till cold. Chop cabbage finely and season with salt and pepper and butter; beat eggs well, then beat them into rich milk—or cream is better. Mix it all together well and bake in a moderate oven till nicely browned.

—Farmer's Wife, Toledo Blade

*Dr. Chase's Third Last and Complete Receipt Book and
Household Physician (Memorial Edition)*, 1903

Chestnut Dressing for Fowl

If you have never tried the chestnut dressing for the turkey, you have a new delicacy to taste.

>a quart of large chestnuts
>hut butter
>salt
>1/4 cup butter
>1 teaspoon salt
>dash of pepper
>2 cups bread crumbs
>a drop or two of onion juice

Cut a gash in one side of each chestnut and shake them in a pan of hut butter for a minute or two, then set them in a hot oven to bake for 5 minutes. Remove the shells and the inner skin and cook them in boiling salted water; drain and pass them through a ricer. Add butter, salt, pepper, bread crumbs moistened with a little hot water, and onion juice.

—*Grayville Cook Book*, 1912

Mushrooms with Brown Sauce

> can of mushrooms
> 1 heaping tablespoon butter
> 1 heaping tablespoon flour
> salt and pepper
> grated nutmeg
> wineglass of sherry or Madeira

Place a can of mushrooms into a saucepan with butter and flour; stir them together over the fire until they begin to brown; gradually stir in the liquor from the can, adding water if any is needed to make the sauce the proper consistency. Add the mushrooms and season the sauce palatably with salt, pepper, and very little grated nutmeg; when the mushrooms are hot, stir in sherry or Madeira and serve the mushrooms as a vegetable.

Toast may be served beneath the mushrooms to increase the size of the dish, or the sauce and mushrooms may be poured on a dish with broiled beefsteak, broiled chicken, or tenderloin of beef.

Stuffed Morels

Morels are a variety of mushroom frequently found under the trees upon old lawns and in rather open woods. After cleansing the morels, cut them at the bottom far enough to admit a force-meat of cold chopped meat and bread, highly seasoned, or of partly cooked sausage. Close them with a sliver of wood or a small metal skewer, lay them on small slices of bread, and place them in a moderate oven to bake for about 10 minutes or until tender. Serve them very hot on toast.

CATSUPS, PICKLES, AND JELLIES

Green Tomato Catsup

- ½ bushel tomatoes
- 1 gallon vinegar
- 1 teacup sugar
- 4 ounces salt
- 3 ounces green peppers
- 1 ounce cinnamon
- ½ ounce ground cloves
- 1 dram cayenne pepper

Slice the tomatoes and stew in their own liquor until soft, then rub through a sieve fine enough to retain seeds and boil the pulp down to the consistency of apply butter (very thick), stirring steadily all the time to prevent burning. Add the vinegar and a small teacup of sugar and the spices, boil up twice, remove from the stove and let cool to bottle. Those who like onions may add a half dozen medium-sized ones peeled and sliced about 15 minutes before the vinegar and spices are put in.

—Mrs. M. M. Munsell, Delaware
Livingston and the Tomato, 1893

French Tomato Pickle

1 peck green tomatoes
6 large onions
1 teacup salt
5 quarts vinegar
2 pounds brown sugar
½ pound white mustard seed
2 tablespoons ground allspice
2 tablespoons cinnamon
2 tablespoons cloves
2 tablespoons ginger
2 tablespoons ground mustard

Slice tomatoes and onions. Mix these and throw salt over them; let them stand overnight. The next day drain thoroughly and boil in one quart vinegar mixed with two quarts of water for 15 or 20 minutes. Then take four quarts vinegar, brown sugar, white mustard seed, ground allspice, cinnamon, cloves, ginger, and ground mustard; throw all together and boil 15 minutes.

—Mrs. President Rutherford B. Hayes

Wild Crabapple Jelly

Cook the crab apples until the skins will peel off, after which remove and punch out core with a goose-quill. To 1 gallon add 1 gallon of cold water; let them soak for 3 days. Then add half as much water as there is liquid; to 2 pints of this add 1 1/4 pints of sugar and boil until it is jelly.

—Mrs. Samuel Woods, Milford Center
Centennial Buckeye Cook Book, 1876

DESSERTS

Hayes Cake

    1 cup sugar
    ½ cup butter
    3 well-beaten eggs
    1 level teaspoon soda
    ½ cup sour mild
    2 small cups flour

Mix all ingredients and flavor with lemon. Pour into small dripping pan and bake half an hour and cut in squares.

—Miss Flora D. Ziegler (nine years old), Columbus
  Centennial Buckeye Cook Book, 1876

Lord Baltimore Cake

    ⅓ cup butter
    1 cup sugar
    8 egg yolks
    ½ cup milk
    1 ¾ cups flour
    4 teaspoons baking powder
    2 teaspoons vanilla

Cream butter and add sugar gradually while beating constantly; then add egg yolks, beaten until thick and lemon-colored; milk; flour, mixed and sifted with baking powder; and vanilla. Bake in 3 buttered and floured 7-inch square tins. Put layers together with Lord Baltimore Filling and cover top and sides with Ice Cream Frosting.

LORD BALTIMORE FILLING. Beat Ice Cream Frosting without flavoring until cold and add ½ cup rolled, dry macaroons, ¼ cup each chopped almonds and pecans, 12 candied cherries cut in quarters, 2 teaspoons lemon juice, 3 teaspoons sherry wine, and ¼ teaspoon orange extract.

ICE CREAM FROSTING. Cook 1½ cups sugar and ½ cup water in a smooth granite-ware saucepan until syrup will spin a long thread when dropped from tip of spoon. Pour gradually, while beating constantly, onto the whites of 2 eggs beaten until stiff (but not dry), add flavoring, and continue the beating until mixture is of the right consistency to spread.

—*Catering for Special Occasions*, 1911

Premium Fruit Cake

If anyone will follow this recipe, she may do as I did—get the first premium at the coming fair.

    3 cups sugar
    1 ½ cups butter
    6 eggs
    1 ½ cups sour cream
    2 teaspoons saleratus or soda
    ½ pound currants
    ¾ pound raisins
    1/4 pound citron
    1 nutmeg
    flour

Beat the eggs thoroughly; then add sugar and butter and beat till smooth. Dissolve the saleratus in a little warm water and put it in the cream; make the cake quite thick with flour to prevent the fruit from settling to the bottom. Do not chop the raisins, but cut them in halves and remove the seeds, else use "seedless" raisins; then scald a few moments to soften, drain and flour (dredge) them before putting into the cake. Cut the citron in thin slices, and as you fill in a layer of cake put the citron over evenly, then more of the cake mixture and another layer of the citron; and so on, until the citron is evenly divided through the whole.

—Mrs. John Rice, Seneca County, Ohio

Dr. Chase's Third Last and Complete Receipt Book and
Household Physician (Memorial Edition), 1903

Mont Blanc Custard

½ box gelatine
3 eggs
2 cups sugar
juice of 2 lemons
1 ½ pints milk

Soak gelatine for half an hour in a half pint of cold water; add a half pint boiling water and, when cool, the whites of three eggs well beaten, sugar, and lemon juice. Beat the whole thoroughly half an hour or more and put away to cool in a mould or in a dozen egg glasses (the latter make a handsome dish and are easier to serve.) Make a boiled custard of the egg yolks and milk; sweeten to taste. Put the dozen snowballs in the glass fruit dish and pour over them the cold custard.

—Miss Lou Brown, Washington City

Centennial Buckeye Cook Book, 1876

Garfield Cookies

1 cup butter
1 cup sugar
⅓ cup sour milk
2 eggs

1 teaspoon soda
½ of a nutmeg grated
flour

Cream the butter and sugar, add the milk, then the eggs, grated nutmeg, and lastly the flour. Turn the mixture on a board lightly sprinkled with flour, roll until very thin, and cut the desired shape and size. Place in slightly greased pan and bake in quick oven.

—*Mrs. Seely's Cook Book*, 1902

Sister Lizzie's Shaker Sugar Pie

2 tablespoons butter
1 cup brown sugar
2 cups light cream
⅓ cup flour
1 teaspoon vanilla
nutmeg
9" unbaked pie shell

Thoroughly mix flour and brown sugar and spread evenly in the bottom of unbaked pie shell. Add cream and vanilla. Slice butter into pieces and distribute evenly over top of pie. Sprinkle with nutmeg and bake in 350 degree oven for 40–45 minutes or until firm.

—The Golden Lamb, Ohio's Oldest Inn, Lebanon, Ohio
    Paul Resetar (Golden Lamb Manager),
    Personal Communication, July 10, 2001

Ohio Shaker Lemon Pie

It's hard to imagine a pie with only three ingredients! But this recipe produces a lemon pie unlike any other you have ever tasted—both tart and sweet at the same time. The real surprise is the pieces of whole lemon in every bite.

2 lemons
2 cups sugar

5 eggs
Pastry for a 2-crust 9" pie

Slice lemons, rind and all, as thin as paper. Place them in a bowl and cover with sugar. Let stand for 2 hours or more. After lemons have mixed with sugar pour beaten eggs over the top. Fill unbaked pie crust with this mixture and cover with top crust. Cut small vents in top crust to let steam escape. Place in preheated 450-degree oven for 15 minutes, then lower temperature to 350 degrees and bake for an additional 30 minutes or until knife inserted comes out clean.

—The Golden Lamb, Ohio's Oldest Inn, Lebanon, Ohio
   Paul Resetar (Golden Lamb Manager),
   Personal Communication, July 10, 2001

Plum Pudding

1 pound marrow or suet
1 pound fine flour dried
8 or 10 eggs
half a nutmeg grated
mace
cinnamon
ginger
a pinch of salt
1 pound currants
1 pound raisins
2 ounces candied citron peel
2 ounces sweet almonds
2 ounces loaf sugar
wineglass of brandy

To make a rich plum pudding, mix well-chopped marrow or suet, flour, well-beaten eggs, nutmeg, mace, cinnamon, and ginger (all powdered very fine), and a pinch of salt, then beat up into a batter. Then add currants and raisins, stoned and chopped a little; the currants should be rubbed in a cloth, and well picked, or well wash and dry them. Add to the batter candied citron peel or part lemon, orange (cut small), sweet almonds (blanched and cut up in bits), grated loaf sugar, and brandy; mix them together. Batter may be boiled in a buttered basin or mould; if the batter should be too stiff, put a glass of white wine in it. It will take 4 or 5 hours' boiling. Strew over it powdered loaf sugar; garnish with sliced lemon.

—*Wright's Book of 3000 Practical Receipts*, 1869

Peach Ice Cream

 1 quart cream
 1 pound powdered sugar
 fresh peaches

Slice the peaches thin and scatter the sugar between the slices. Cover it and let the fruit steep 3 hours. Then cut or chop it up in the syrup and strain it through a hair sieve or bag of double coarse lace. Beat gradually into the cream and freeze as rapidly as possible. It is very nice with 2 or 3 handfuls of freshly cut bits of the fruit stirred in when the cream is half frozen.

—*Common Sense in the Household*, 1871

Butterscotch

 3 cups brown sugar
 ¾ cup water
 butter the size of a walnut
 pinch of soda
 flavor to suit the taste

Cook all ingredients till they begin to harden when dripping from a spoon. Pour mixture out into buttered pie pans. As it cools, mark it off in squares with a knife dipped in water to keep it from sticking. When wanted for eating, turn the pan bottom side up, knock on it, and the candy will come out without any trouble.

—Lizzie Mast, Springfield

 The Housekeepers New Cook Book, 1883

Cream Candy

Mix 3 cups of white sugar with a little more water than enough to cover. Don't stir it while it's cooking. Let it boil till it ropes, then before taking it off the stove add a teaspoon of cream of tartar moistened with the flavoring you choose. When cold, pull until perfectly white.
—Mrs. Lizzie K., Springfield
The Housekeepers New Cook Book, 1883

BEVERAGES

Toasted Coffee

Wash and pick the coffee; put it in a very large stove pan in a hot oven. Stir often, giving constant attention. It must be toasted the darkest brown, yet not one grain must be burned. It should never be glazed, as this destroys the aroma. Two pints of coffee become three pints after toasting.
—*Practical American Cookery*, 1885

Chocolate Cocoa Nibs or Shells

    1 quart boiling water
    2 ounces cocoa nibs
    1 quart fresh milk

Wet the shells or nibs up with a little cold water. Add to the boiling water and cook an hour and a half. Strain and add the milk; let it heat almost to boiling, then take from the fire.
—*Common Sense in the Household*, 1871

Barley Water

> 2 tablespoons pearl barley
> 3 or 4 lumps of sugar
> pinch or 2 of salt
> strip of lemon peel

Wipe the pearl barley very clean. Put it in a quart jug with the sugar, salt, and strip of lemon peel. Fill up the jug with boiling water and shake the mixture gently for some minutes. Then cover it and let it stand until perfectly cold. In 12 hours it will be fit for use. Made in this way the barley water will be comparatively clear and soft and pleasant to drink. If the flavor of lemon is unpalatable, or sugar makes it too sweet, these ingredients may be omitted or modified.

Innocent Wine

Pick from their stalks fine grapes of either the Concord, Diana, Delaware, or Muscatel variety. Lay them in a strong straining cloth in an earthen dish or jar and bruise or break them, with a wood masher preferably. Hang them in the cloth to drain and squeeze out all the juice, which will carry with it a portion of the colored tissue lying next to the skin and holding the delicious aroma of the grape. Stir in liquid sugar to sweeten it. Take special care that you do not get it too sweet—that is a fault of inexperienced cooks and of the untried palate. Melt the sugar thin with fresh cold water. In adding the water use judgment; the proportion is sometimes a third part of water. Set the mixture on ice and serve ice-cold in a glass pitcher containing ice. This is a wholesome and delicious afternoon-tea drink taken with biscuit slightly sweetened.

—*Mrs. Seely's Cook Book*, 1902

My Dear Sir:

In reply to your question as to the use of wine at public and large private dinners, I am not confident that there is any marked decline in the practice of placing it on the table at such banquets. But if my observation is correct, the number of those who decline to partake of it is increasing, and the number of those who drink to intoxication, even in the slightest degree, is less than it was a few years ago.

> Sincerely,
> Rutherford B. Hayes,
> Spiegel Grove
> —From an April 17, 1891 diary entry

A Bishop

    cloves
    lemon or orange rind
    cinnamon
    allspice
    mace
    nutmeg
    Port or claret wine
    sugar

Stick cloves in the rind of a lemon or orange and roast it a long time before a slow fire. Put equal quantities of cinnamon, cloves, allspice, and mace into a little water, and boil them until the whole strength is extracted. Boil a bottle of Port or claret wine and put the roast lemon and spice into it. Sweeten, and add the juice of half a lemon and grate in some nutmeg. Serve hot with lemon and spice floating in it.

—*Mrs. Seely's Cook Book*, 1902

Hot Coffee and Soda

   ¼ pound of good coffee
   ¼ ounce of ground chicory
   soda water
   cream syrup or condensed milk and sugar

For temperance advocates, hot black coffee mixed with soda water is a good substitute for the spirituous winter drinks. Make black coffee as follows: the coffee and ground chicory infused in a quart of boiling water, but not boiled, will make medium strong coffee. Boiling coffee makes it very black and bitter. Use hot black coffee and soda water in equal proportions, with a palatable addition of cream syrup or condensed milk and sugar.

—*Practical American Cookery*, 1885

Recommendation for Coffee

The recipes in this book can be filled to great advantage and entire satisfaction by using the Neptune Brand of Roasted Coffee. It is an elegant coffee, perfectly roasted, nicely and conveniently packed in one pound packages for choice family use, for sale by grocers throughout Ohio. The Neptune Brand is prepared only by John H. Gause & Co. at the Lake Shore Mills, Cleveland, Ohio.

—Advertisement in the *Centennial Buckeye Cook Book*, 1876

Acorn Coffee

Take sound ripe acorns, peel them, and roast them with a little butter or fat. When cold, grind them with ⅓ their weight of real coffee.

—*Wright's Book of 3000 Practical Receipts*, 1869

Almond Milk

    1 ounce sweet almonds
    3 bitter almonds
    1 ½ pound white sugar
    2 pints clear water
    orange-flower water

Blanch the almonds by steeping them in hot water for a little time, then beat them up in a mortar with the sugar and add the water gradually. Lastly, strain and add the flavoring.

—*Wright's Book of 3000 Practical Receipts*, 1869

PART SIX: Appendix

Miscellaneous Recipes and Remedies

CHAPTER ONE

RECEIPTS FOR GROOMING THE BODY

Skin and Face

TO KEEP HANDS SOFT AND WHITE. A French receipt for this purpose is to sleep in gloves filled with a paste made of half a pound of soft soap, a gill of salad oil, and an ounce of mutton tallow. Boil together until thoroughly incorporated. As soon as this is done boiling, but before cold, add one gill of spirits of wine and a grain of musk. This is a rather troublesome process, but the result is entirely satisfactory.

TO CURE MOIST HANDS. Some people have moist, clammy hands that are disagreeable to the touch. Exercise, plain living, and the local application of starch powder and lemon juice will cure this affliction.

TO WHITEN ARMS. For an evening party or theatricals, rub arms with glycerine, and before the skin has absorbed it all, dust on refined chalk.

TO REMOVE TAR FROM SKIN. Tar can be instantly removed from the fingers by rubbing them with the outside of a fresh orange or lemon peel and wiping them dry immediately afterward. It is astonishing what a small piece will clean. The volatile oils in the skin dissolve the tar, so it can be wiped off.

TO REMOVE SKIN TAN. An elegant preparation for removing tan is made of one-half pint new milk, one-quarter ounce lemon juice, and one-half ounce white brandy. Boil all together and remove the scum. Use night and morning.

TO REMOVE PIMPLES. If you have blackheads or flesh worms, common flour of sulphur will remove them. Wash the face with soap, dry thoroughly, and rub the sulphur into the skin with soft flannel, taking care not to get any into the eyes; two or three applications will remove them with a very little pressure. Use a watch key pressing over the obstinate places and wash off again with warm suds. If the pores of the skin are large, use the sulphur once a week. It is an excellent remedy for spots on the face or scars. Bathe very often; a sponge bath should be taken every night if possible. A good diet is to be preferred to medicines. Oranges, apples, figs, and prunes all can be readily obtained; pork should not be used nor much butter when one has a coarse, pimply skin.

TO REMOVE FRECKLES. Many ladies are very much annoyed at freckles; but we have seen faces on which they were positive beautifiers. Probably the best eradicator of these little blemishes is known as "Unction de Maintenon," composed of Venice soap dissolved in lemon juice, with oil of bitter almonds and deliquidated oil of tartar, and after it has turned to ointment in the sun, oil of rhodium. Bathe the freckled face at night with this lotion and wash it in the morning with clear, cold water or, if convenient, with a wash of elder flower and rose water. A little lemon juice and milk mixed together and applied nightly will also remove freckles.

TO MAKE COLD CREAM (WHICH ALSO REMOVES FRECKLES). To an ounce of white wax melted in a clean dish, put one cup fresh lard, half a teaspoon of pulverized gum camphor, and a teaspoon of glycerine;

stir well and pour into cups or other molds that have been dipped into cold water. When solid, turn out and wrap in tin foil.

To Fortify Against Wrinkles. The hand of time cannot be stayed, but his marks upon the face need not be placed there prematurely. One of the best local treatments consists in bathing the skin frequently in cold water and then rubbing with a towel until the flesh is aglow. A little bran added to the water is a decided improvement. This treatment stimulates the functions of the skin and gives it vigor. The wrinkling may be further remedied by washing the parts three times a day with a mix of 4 drams of glycerine, 2 drams of tannin, 2 drams of rectified spirits, and 8 ounces of water.

To Relieve Barber's Itch and Other Sores of a Chronic and Malignant Character. Mrs. H. J. Merrill of Toledo, Ohio, gave me the following, which she has used many years with great success on all bad sores of longstanding and of an irritable character:

> 2 tablespoons gunpowder, sulphur, and alum each, powdered
> ½ pint unsalted lard or fresh unsalted butter

Put into an earthen dish and stew on the back of the stove for 24 hours, strain and box for use. Cleanse the sore well with warm castile soap suds, dry carefully with soft cloths, and apply sparingly at first, as it will "bite," to show its power over the disease.

To Relieve Itching or Prurigo. My old friend, Dr. T. B. King, of Toledo, Ohio, mixes the following:

> 1 ounce oxide of zinc ointment
> 20 grams camphor gum, ground to a fine powder
> a few drops of alcohol
> 12 to 15 grams red precipitate

Rub a little of the ointment upon the parts, and if a fold of the skin or flesh comes together and chafes, put a little of the ointment upon a soft cloth and put between. It soon relieves.

Hair

TO CLEANSE THE HAIR. Break the whites of two eggs into a basin of soft water and work them up to a froth in the roots of the hair. Rinse thoroughly with clean warm water.

TO REMOVE A MOUSTACHE. A broken Florence flask is needed, because water will boil in it; put a little powder in the glass, add some water, and apply a lighted candle under the glass. When it begins to get hot, invert a funnel over the steam and hold your moustache over the end of the funnel, so the steam may reach the hair without touching the eyes. The fumes are injurious to the eyes. Now apply the mixture very lightly to the moustache while it is still as warm as you can bear; when it is dry, wet it and wash it off. When the moustache is very heavy there will be a down show in two or three weeks; take a pair of tweezers and remove it.

TO PREVENT FALLING HAIR AND TO REMOVE DANDRUFF. A hairwash for keeping the hair from falling and cleansing it of dandruff is sold by the perfumers and is made as follows: Take a half pound castor oil, a half pint strongest alcohol, 48 grains powdered cantharides, a half ounce oil of bergamot, and 4 drops attar of roses. Mix, let stand for seven days, frequently shaking, and then filter and keep in well-closed bottles.

TO WARD OFF GRAY HAIR. We can only counsel moderation in all those pleasures that tend to an exciting, unhealthy mode of living, but here is a receipt that a writer says she believes will prevent graying: melt 4 ounces of pure hog's lard (unsalted) and 4 drams of spermaceti together; when cool add 4 drams of oxide of bismuth. Perfume to suit yourself. Use as a dressing.

TO PREVENT BALDNESS. Feather pillows, by conforming to the shape of the head, prevent ventilation and tend to overheat the scalp. This weakens it and may lead to premature baldness or other affliction. Curled hair should be substituted for feathers whenever possible.

To Cure Baldness. The celebrated Baron Dupuytren's pomade, a receipt known for many years, has found a prominent place in the list of remedies for this evil. Leave 6 ounces of boxwood shavings to steep for 14 days at 60 degrees temperature in 12 ounces of proof spirit. Strain off the liquid and add 2 ounces of spirits of rosemary and 2 ounces of spirits of nutmeg. Rub this thoroughly on the bald spots, night and morning.

Teeth

To Care for the Teeth. Salt and water cure tender gums. In the early stages, vinegar will remove tartar, but if it remains too long it has a tendency to loosen the teeth. Never use a pin or any metal substance to remove food that lodges between the teeth. Food and drinks that are too hot or too cold will destroy the beauty of the teeth.

To Cure Foul Breath. A gargle made of a spoonful of chloride of lime dissolved in a half tumbler of water will sweeten the breath. Bad breath also can be rendered less disagreeable by rinsing the mouth with Horsford's Acid Phosphate.

To Cure Specific Odors. We wish there were some law to prevent people from polluting their breaths with onions and tobacco when they are going into mixed company. No one has a right to make himself in any manner offensive to others. All the laws of good breeding forbid it. The taint of smoking can be overcome by chewing common parsley. The odor imparted to the breath by garlic and onions may be very much diminished by chewing roasted coffee grains or parsley leaves and seeds.

Soap, Cologne, and Powder

To Make Fine Cologne Water. Into a bottle, drop the following oils: 1 dram each of lavender and bergamot, 2 drams each of lemon and rosemary, 8 drams each of cinnamon and cloves, and 50 drams of tincture of musk. Cork and shake well.

TO MAKE VIOLET POWDER. Take 12 pounds of wheat starch and 2 pounds of powdered orris; mix together and add one-half ounce attar of lemon and 2 drams each attars of bergamot and cloves.

TO MAKE LYE. Boil for six hours ten gallons of lye made of green wood ashes. Add eight or ten pounds of grease you have saved from the kitchen and continue to boil. If thick or ropy, add more lye till the grease is absorbed; this is ascertained by dropping a spoonful in a glass of water, and if grease remains it will show on the water.

TO MAKE HARD SOAP. Pour four gallons boiling water onto six pounds of washing soda and three pounds of unslaked lime. Let it stand until perfectly clear, then drain off the water. Put in six pounds clean fat. Boil until it begins to harden—about two hours—stirring most of the time. While boiling, thin with two gallons of cold water, which you have poured on the alkaline mixture after draining off the four gallons. This must also settle clear before it is drawn off. Add it when there is danger of boiling over. Try the thickness by cooling a little on a plate. Put in a handful of salt just before taking from the fire. Wet a tub to prevent sticking; turn in the soap and let it stand until solid. Cut into bars; put on a board and let it dry. This will make about 40 pounds of nice soap, much better for washing (when it has dried out for 2 or 3 months) than yellow turpentine soap.

TO MAKE SOFT SOAP. Let ten pounds of grease, six pounds of washing soda, and eight gallons of hot water stand for several days until the grease is eaten up. If too thick, add more water. Stir every day. If wood ashes are used instead of soda, boil the mixture.

CHAPTER TWO

REMEDIES FOR ILLNESS

Discontented Babies

TO SOOTHE THE TEETHING BABY. For the sleeplessness, irritability, and discomfort which so often accompany teething, much can be done by the mother:

☞ A hot foot bath will often have a soothing effect by relieving the congestion in the head and mouth. Mustard can be added with benefit.

☞ A good movement of the bowels, induced with castor oil, will relieve congestion in the gums.

☞ The mother's finger dipped in syrup of lettuce can be gently carried over the tender and inflamed gum and, now and then, by a little firmer pressure, may allow the point of the tooth to free its way.

☞ Make a dried-flour preparation by tying one cup of flour into a stout muslin bag and dropping it into cold water. Then set over the fire. Boil three hours steadily. Turn out the flour ball and dry in the hot sun all day; or, if you need it at once, dry in a moderate oven without shutting the door. To use it, grate a tablespoon for a cup of boiling milk and water (half and half). Wet up the flour with a very little cold water; stir in and boil five minutes. Put in a little salt.

To Soothe Colicky Babies:

※ For colic that may come from cold hands and feet keep a flannel belly band on the baby in both summer and winter.

※ Colic is often due to constipation, in which case an enema of warm water—with the addition of salt at the rate of a level teaspoon to the pint—is required followed by one or two teaspoons of castor oil or other gentle laxative medicine.

※ Paregoric, whisky, brandy, or soothing syrup are improper remedies for colic. Drugging the baby into insensibility or making it drunk will not remove the cause of illness. Colic is often a symptom of some other condition, so this condition should be ascertained and treated.

Sick Children

To Prevent Croup. Take two skeins of black sewing silk, braid them together so they will wear well, and tie loosely around the neck so it will go below the clothes out of sight; and the child will never have the croup while it is worn. Now, some will laugh at this and call it an old woman's notion, but as it costs but little and can do no harm, if you will only try it, you will save the little ones lots of misery and yourselves many a sleepless night.

To Treat Croup. The instant croupy threatenings are observed, keep the child shut indoors and serve very light food indeed—and not much of that—until the symptoms have abated. Put a mustard plaster on the windpipe and let it redden the skin, but not blister. Put the feet in mustard water as hot as they can bear it. Then wipe them dry and keep them covered warm. Croup requires very prompt treatment; if home treatment does not relieve, send immediately for a physician.

To Relieve a Toothache. Cut a large raisin open, roast it or heat it, and apply it around the tooth while it is as hot as can be borne. It will operate like a little poultice and will draw out the inflammation.

To Prevent Scarlet Fever. Give the child, in a dose of as many drops as his years, mixture of three grains extract belladonna (pure), one dram cinnamon water, and seven drams distilled water. Label as poison.

To Relieve Chilblains. Rub well on the feet, nights and mornings, two teaspoons of powdered muriate of ammonia dissolved in one pint of water. Never let a chilblain become a sore but tend to it as soon as the painful itching commences.

Ailing Adults

To Remedy Almost Anything. Break an egg. Separate the yolk and white. Whip each to a stiff froth. Add a tablespoon of arrowroot and a little water to the yolk. Rub till smooth and free of lumps. Pour slowly into half a pint of boiling water, stirring all the time. Let it simmer till jelly-like. Sweeten to the taste and add a tablespoon of French brandy. Stir in the frothed white and drink hot in winter. In summer, set on ice, then stir in the beaten white. Milk may be used instead of water.

To Bind a Cut. Dissolve ocean salt in a pitcher of water and rub this on the flesh with a sponge or apply cobwebs and brown sugar or the dust of tea, applied with laudanum.

To Treat a Burn or Scald. Cover it with wet linen cloths, pouring on more water without removing them till the pain is alleviated, when pure hog's lard may be applied. Or apply lather of soap from the shaving cup with the brush to produce relief. White of egg applied in the same way is also a simple and useful dressing. If the shock is great and there is no reaction, administer frequently aromatic of ammonia or a little brandy and water till the patient rallies.

To Treat Stings. Apply soda, hartshorn, or arnica to the stings of insects, wasps, hornets, and bees. Parsley leaves, applied as a fomentation, will cure the bites or stings of insects.

To Treat Venomous Bites. Apply a moderately tight ligature above the bite of a snake. Wash the wound freely with water to encourage bleeding and then cauterize thoroughly. Afterwards apply lint dipped in equal parts of olive oil and spirits hartshorn; swallow ten drops dissolved in a wineglass of water.

To Cure Headache. The fresh juice of ground ivy snuffed up the nose; ginger powder, formed into a plaster with warm water and applied on paper or cloth to the forehead; mustard poultice applied to the nape of the neck; or a footbath, taken for the purpose of drawing the blood from the head, can also relieve aching of the head.

To Cure Obesity. Fat people may reduce their flesh rapidly by drinking sassafras tea, either cold or hot, with or without sugar. There are conditions of health when it might be injurious, however, and a physician should be consulted before using it. A strong infusion may be made of one ounce of sassafras to a quart of water.

Chlorine Water a Specific for Diphtheria

Springfield Republican. A recent breaking out of diphtheria in a considerable number of places was alarming in its fatality. Some remedies have entirely divested this fearful disease of its terrors if applied in the early stages. Among these the most simple and effective is chlorine water, diluted by adding two to four times the amount of water. A well-known physician of Springfield has used this specific conclusively for 15 years with complete success, previous to its use having lost about half his cases. He repeatedly, by its use, eradicated the disease in different places, when all other remedies failed. Give one to two teaspoons, largely diluted with water, two or three times daily.

—Dr. Chase's Third Last and Complete
Receipt Book and Household Physician, 1903

To Relieve Testicular Pain. The constant use of an elm bark poultice, regularly changed every four hours, will be found a superior remedy for the excruciating pains of the testes which accompany the spread of mumps, whether of recent or long standing

To Allay Nausea. Cloves may be used to allay vomiting and sickness to stomach, to stimulate the digestive functions, improve the flavor or operation of other remedies, and prevent a tendency to their producing sickness or griping.

To Cure Seasickness. 10 to 12 drops of chloroform cures seasickness. One dose cures 18 out of 20; the second cures the others. It is simple, easily obtained, and not unpleasant to take in a little water. And a lady who has had considerable experience in crossing parts of Lake Erie informs me that the smelling of chloroform a few times has relieved much of the nausea attending seasickness. So, also, my judgment is that the taking and inhaling a little of it from the bottle will do great good.

To Remove Iron and Steel from Eyes. Accidents are often occurring to millers, while picking the millstones, by a small bit of steel from the pick penetrating into the coating of the eye. Dr. T. B. King of Toledo informs me that he has cured several cases by putting one or two drops of the following solution into the eye a few times, whereby the steel or iron will be loosened in 24 hours. Then let no one fail to try it, as soon as needed:

> 2 grams iodine,
> 12 grams iodide of potash
> 3 ounces soft water

To Relieve Dysentery. Steep black or green tea in boiling water and sweeten with loaf sugar.

To Relieve Constipation. Castor oil is frequently used to relieve constipation. One part oil of turpentine mixed with three or four parts castor oil increases its purgative effect. The greatest objections to this cathartic are its nauseous taste and its tendency to cause sickness or unconquerable disgust. This may be overcome by adding one ounce of sassafras oil to one pint of castor oil; the dose of this may be given in sweetened water. Any other aromatic oils will answer equally as well.

To Remedy Dyspepsia:

⚜ *Before breakfast.* Rise early, dress warmly, and go out. If strong, walk; if weak, saunter; drink cold water three times. Of all cold baths this is the best for the dyspeptic; after half an hour, come in for breakfast.

⚜ *Breakfast.* For breakfast slowly eat a piece of good steak half as large as your hand, a slice of coarse bread, and a baked apple; talk pleasantly with neighbors; avoid hot biscuits and strong coffee; drink nothing.

⚜ *Work in open air.* Digest for an hour, and then to your work; I trust it is in the open air. Work hard till noon, and then rest body and mind till dinner, sleep a little; drink water.

⚜ *Dinner.* For dinner at two or three o'clock eat a slice of beef, mutton, or fish as large as your hand, a potato, two or three spoonfuls of other vegetables, and a slice of coarse bread; give more than half an hour to this meal; use no drink.

⚜ *After dinner.* After dinner play anaconda for an hour.

⚜ *Supper.* Forgo it. Even a little tea and toast will slow your recovery.

⚜ *Bedtime.* In a warm room bathe your skin with cold water hastily; go to bed in a well-ventilated room before nine o'clock. Follow this prescription for three months and your stomach will so far recover that you can indulge for some time in all sorts of irregular and gluttonous eating; or if you have resolved, in the fear of Heaven, to present your body as a living sacrifice unto God, continue to eat and work like a Christian, and your distressing malady will soon be forgotten.

To Relieve Coughs. Boil one ounce licorice root in one-half pint of water till reduced one-half. Then add one ounce gum arabic and one ounce loaf sugar. Take a teaspoon every few hours. Or, boil three lemons for 15 minutes. Slice them thin while hot over one pound of loaf sugar. Put on the fire in a porcelain-lined saucepan and stew till the syrup is quite thick. After taking it from the fire, add one tablespoon of oil of sweet almonds. Stir till mixed and cool. Take one spoonful or more when the cough is troublesome.

Colds and Inflammation—Health Rules for Winter

- Never lean with the back upon anything that is cold.
- Never begin a journey until the breakfast has been eaten.
- Never take warm drinks and then immediately go out in the cold air.
- Keep the back, especially between the shoulders, well covered; also the chest well protected.
- Never go to bed with cold or damp feet; always toast them by a fire 10 or 15 minutes before going to bed.
- Never omit weekly bathing; unless the skin is active, the cold will close the pores and favor congestion or other diseases.
- After exercise, never ride in an open carriage or near the window of a car for a moment; it is dangerous to health and even to life.
- Warm the back by a fire, and never continue keeping the back exposed to heat after it has become comfortably warm; to do otherwise is debilitating.
- When going from a warm atmosphere into a colder one, keep the mouth closed so that the air may be warmed by its passage through the nose ere it reaches the lungs.
- Never stand still in cold weather, especially after having taken a slight degree of exercise, and always avoid standing on ice or snow or where you're exposed to cold wind; in short, keep your feet warm, your head cool, and your mouth shut and you will seldom "catch cold."

—Common Sense in the
Household, 1871

TO TREAT ENLARGED TONSILS. Take one or two daily applications of lemon juice with a camel's hair pencil.

TO RELIEVE PLEURISY. Prepare a mustard plaster from equal parts of wheaten or rye flour and lukewarm or cold water, spread upon fabric, and apply with a thin tissue, as of gauze, intervening between the plaster and skin.

TO TREAT ACUTE CARDIAC PAIN. Whether or not due to angina pectoris, a mustard plaster will relieve you.

TO CURE BACKACHES. Many young girls and older women suffer from headache, dizziness, sluggishness of thought and disposition to sleep, with pains in the back and lower limbs and general nervousness and irritability. All of these symptoms are indications of diseased kidneys.

Mrs. Jolly of Cleveland, Ohio, writes:

I have taken nearly two boxes of Dr. Parker's Sure Kidney Cure and will say that they have helped me very much. Before taking your pills it was impossible for me to lie still one hour at night with the pain in my back. Now I do not feel any pain unless I do a washing or walk a long distance. I shall continue to take your Kidney Pills until entirely cured.

—*Sloan's Cook Book and Advice to Housekeepers,* 1905

TO FACILITATE CHILDBIRTH. Some physicians consider drinking half a pint of elm bark powder boiled in a pint of new milk daily, during and after the seventh month of gestation, as advantageous in facilitating and causing an easy delivery.

Other Conditions and Cures

Other substances with the ability to heal various conditions:

❋ *Ginger* is eminently useful in habitual flatulence, atonic dyspepsia, hysteria, and enfeebled and relaxed habits, especially of old and gouty individuals.

❀ The power of *lemonade* in preventing and arresting scurvy is unequaled by any other remedy, except a liberal supply of fresh vegetables of the cruciform family.

❀ *Ivy leaves* have been efficient in diseases of the skin, indolent ulcers, eczemas, and itch in the form of decoction applied locally; this will also destroy vermin in the hair, which, it is stated, is stained black by the application.

❀ A *cataplasm of onions* pounded with vinegar, applied for a number of days, and changed three times a day, has been found to cure corns and bunions.

❀ *Sage* is a valuable anaphrodisiac to check excessive venereal desires. It may be used in connection with moral, hygienic, and other aids, if necessary.

❀ *Vanilla* is an aromatic stimulant said to exhilarate the brain, prevent sleep, increase muscular energy, and stimulate the sexual propensities. It is also considered an aphrodisiac and is much used in perfumery and to flavor tinctures, syrups, ointments, and confectionery.

❀ *Nutmeg* is recommended for the cure of fever. Char a nutmeg by holding it to the flame and permitting it to burn by itself without disturbance; when charred, pulverize it, combine it with an equal quantity of burnt alum, and divide the mixture into three powders. On the commencement of the chill, give a powder. If this does not break it, give the second powder on the approach of the next chill; and if not cured, give the third powder as the succeeding chill comes on.

❀ *Mistletoe* has been beneficially employed in epilepsy, hysteria, insanity, paralysis, and other nervous diseases. In using this agent, it is always necessary to regulate the condition of the stomach and bowels, the menstrual discharge and other faulty secretions, and remove worms, if present, previous to its exhibition.

❀ *Passionflower* is especially useful to allay restlessness and overcome wakefulness, when these are the result of exhaustion or the nervous excitement of debility. It proves especially useful in the insomnia of infants and old people. The sleep induced by passiflora is a peaceful, restful slumber, and the patient awakens quiet and refreshed.

CHAPTER THREE

$\mathcal{H}$OUSEHOLD RECEIPTS

Remedies for Household Pests

❧ Dissolve one ounce corrosive sublimate in one pint strong spirits. Put it on the bedsteads, and it will destroy the bedbugs and their eggs. Two ounces commercial carbolic acid will greatly improve the mixture.

❧ Cayenne pepper will keep the storeroom and pantry free from ants and cockroaches.

❧ For bugs and ants, dissolve two pounds alum in three quarts boiling water. Apply boiling hot with a brush. Add alum to whitewash for storerooms, pantries, and closets.

❧ Kerosene oil is a sure remedy for red ants. Place small blocks under a sugar barrel, so as not to let the oil touch the barrel.

❧ Uncork a bottle of oil of pennyroyal, and it will drive away mosquitoes or other blood-sucking insects.

❧ Mix a little powdered potash with meal and throw it into the rat holes and it will not fail to drive the rats away.

❧ If a mouse enters into any part of your dwelling, saturate a rag with cayenne in solution and stuff it into his hole.

Cleaning and Polishing Furniture and Utensils

To Clean Copper Ware. Wash and rub with half a lemon. Take a handful of common salt and enough vinegar and flour to make a paste; mix together thoroughly. There is nothing better for cleaning coppers. After using the paste, wash thoroughly with hot water, rinse in cold water, and wipe dry.

To Clean Glassware. Fill with buttermilk, let stand 48 hours, and wash in soapsuds. Or, put in two tablespoons of vinegar and a tablespoon of baking soda. This will effervesce vigorously. Hold the article over the sink; if a decanter, do not cork or the vessel may burst.

To Remove the Yellow Discoloration of China. Moisten a soft cloth in water and dip into dry salt or fine coal or wood ashes and rub off the stain with it. Afterwards wash with soap and water.

Clean windows with a chamois

To Clean Draperies. Draperies and tapestries hung upon the walls may be cleaned by pouring gasoline into a shallow pan and brushing them with this by means of a soft brush or whisk broom.

To Polish Hard-Wood Floors. Chip up fine not quite half a pound of beeswax and put it on the stove to melt. When melted, pour it in one quart of turpentine and add five cents' worth of ammonia. Then set it in a tin pail of hot water and stir the polish over the fire until thoroughly blended. Remember that all these ingredients are highly flammable and guard against their taking fire. See that the hard-wood floor is perfectly clean, dry, and free from dust; then apply the polish to it with a soft woolen cloth, rubbing it well into the grain of the wood; after the polish is applied to the floor, rub it very hard with a polishing brush, which can be found at the house-furnishing shops. Hard-wood floors require polishing two or three times a week.

TO POLISH FURNITURE. Mix one pint of alcohol, one pint of spirits of turpentine, one and one-half pint of raw linseed oil, one ounce balsam fir, and one ounce ether. Cut the balsam with the alcohol, which will take about 12 hours. (That is to say, dilute the balsam with the alcohol.) Mix the oil with the turpentine in a separate vessel and add the alcohol, and last the ether. Apply with a woolen cloth.

Clothing

TO CLEAN LACE. Stretch the lace carefully on a thick piece of wrapping paper, fastening the edges with pins. Sprinkle it quite thickly with calcinated magnesia, cover with another piece of wrapping paper, and place it under a pile of books or other heavy weight for three or four days. The magnesia can then be shaken off and the lace will appear like new. It will not only be clean, but the edges will be in perfect condition. Calcinated magnesia is very cheap, and this method is well worth trying.

TO CLEAN DARK OR SOBER-COLORED SILK. Mix together two cups cold water, one tablespoon honey, one pound soft soap, and one wineglass alcohol. Shake up well. Lay the silk, a breadth at a time, on a table, and sponge both sides with this, rubbing it in well; shake it about well and up and down in a tub of cold water; flap it as dry as you can, but do not wring it. Hang it by the edges, not the middle, until fit to iron.

To Clean Crepe, Mourning, and Other Black Goods. Black dress goods may be washed by observing the same caution as for other colored fabrics, whether cotton, linen, wool, or silk. Use two tablespoons of ammonia to a half-gallon of water. Take a piece of black cloth and sponge off with the preparation and afterward with clean water. Iron while damp on the wrong side, or that which is to be inside when the stuff is made up.

Recommendation for Cleaning Fine Clothes

Mohairs and such hard stuffs do not color or clean well by the old process; consequently, they should be cleaned by the new French dry process so that a good finish can be guaranteed.

Professor William B. Tarr, Chemical Dyer, has fitted up steam machinery and appliances in his Springfield, Ohio, establishment to enable him to do first-class work. Professor Tarr will have exclusive control of all fine work, such as ladies dresses and new goods requiring the color changed. He colors and cleans all silks, woolens, and mixed goods. Ribbons, neck ties, and kid gloves are artistically and successfully cleaned and dyed.

The professor, having spent three years in China, learned the process of cleaning and restoring gentlemen's clothing without dipping the garment, thereby securing against any possible chance of shrinkage. With this assurance gentlemen can, with full confidence, take in their fine coats, pants, and vests and have them renovated in first-class style.

—Advertisement in *Centennial Buckeye Cook Book,* 1876

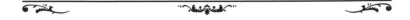

To Tend Stains. The principal stains and spots the laundress has to do with are tea, coffee, wine, iron rust, ink, paint, tar, grass, mildew, blood, grease, and mud stains. These should all be removed from washable articles before sending them to the laundry. Hence many housekeepers set apart Tuesday for wash day, and take occasion Monday to sort the wash and carefully remove all stains, and sponge or scrub or dry-clean any articles that may require it.

To Remove Tea and Coffee Stains. When fresh, these yield readily to the action of boiling water, especially if the fabric be stretched tightly and the boiling water poured upon it with some force. If stains have been neglected and fixed by soap in the laundry, it may be necessary to treat them with lemon juice and salt, afterwards exposing the article to the air and sunshine.

Recommendation for Washing Clothes

If I were to be asked, by one who was a beginner, what in my judgment was the best way to secure peace, long life, and happiness in the family, I would first ask, "Have you a clothes wringer?" If not, I would then be ready to give my advice. Taking care to let conscience rule, I would say, "Get as one of the first and most essential things Way's Patent Lever Clothes Wringer," and then give my reasons, which are many:

1. It is the most durable and simple in its construction.
2. Its superiority of rolls.
3. No thumb screws, cogs, or springs to rust and get out of order.
4. Its rolls adjust themselves to any thickness of cloth, from a bed quilt to the thinnest lace, merely by the pressure of the foot.
5. Your tub cannot tip over as it is not fastened to the wringer, but on one of the best commodities that can grace a laundry, a bench neat and handy, so that a child can readily work it.

In fact, time nor space would allow the naming of all there is to be said in praise of this, the woman's friend. It has taken the premium and two prize medals at the Cincinnati Exposition, 1873–1874 and first premium at the State Fairs of Ohio. In fact it gives splendid satisfaction. Everybody likes it. It is the common sense wringer.

—Advertisement in *Centennial Buckeye Cook Book,* 1876

To Remove Iron-Gall Inks, Tea, Red Wine, and Fruit. When stains are fresh they may be removed by dipping immediately in warm water or warm milk; when they are more stubborn, they may require soaking in buttermilk for some time, the action being strong in proportion as the liquid sours with age. The addition of common salt increases effectiveness.

To Remove Grease Stains. Various absorbents are recommended to remove grease from fabrics. Among the most useful of these are brown paper and blotting paper. Others are chalk, French chalk (which is not chalk but ground soapstone), pipe clay, fuller's earth, magnesia, gypsum, common starch, and melted tallow.

To Remove Blood Stains. Use cornstarch.

BIBLIOGRAPHY

BOOKS AND ARTICLES

A Lady of Charleston. *The Carolina Housewife or House and Home.* Charleston, S.C.: W.R. Babcock & Co, 1847.

"Bathing," *Peterson's Magazine,* June 1872. At: American Federation of Old West Re-Enactors (see websites).

Beebe, Katherine. *Home Occupations for Little Children.* Chicago: The Werner Company, 1896.

Beecher, Catherine E., and Harriet Beecher Stowe. *The American Woman's Home, or Principles of Domestic Science.* New York: J.B. Ford, 1869.

Boda, A.Z. *Visitors Guide to Columbus.* Columbus, Ohio: A.Z. Boda, 1880.

"Calling Card Etiquette," *The Delineator.* At: Victoriana.Com (see websites).

Carnegie, Andrew. "Wealth." *North American Review,* CXLVIII, no. 391 (June 1889), 653-64. At: Internet Modern History Sourcebook (see websites).

Carter, Mary Elizabeth. *Millionaire Households and Their Domestic Economy: With Hints upon Fine Living.* New York: D. Appleton & Co, 1903.

Chase, A.W., M.D. *Dr. Chase's Third Last and Complete Receipt Book and Household Physician (Memorial Edition).* Detroit: F.B. Dickerson Company, 1903.

Corson, Juliet. *Miss Corson's Practical American Cookery and Household Management.* New York: Dodd, Mead, and Company, 1885.

Craik, Dinah Maria Mulock. *A Woman's Thoughts About Women*. London: Hurst and Blackett, 1858. At: Victorian Women Writers Project (see websites).

Crane, Rev. Jonathan Townley. *Popular Amusements*. Cincinnati: Hitchcock and Walden, 1870. At: Making of America (see websites).

Dick & Fitzgerald. *Athletic Sports for Boys: A Repository of Graceful Recreations for Youth*. New York: Dick & Fitzgerald, 1866. At: Making of America (see websites).

Eaton, Seymour. *One Hundred Lessons in Business*. Boston: Seymour Eaton, 1887.

Farmer, Fannie Merritt. *Catering for Special Occasions*. Philadelphia: David McKay, 1911.

Farmer, Fannie Merritt. *The Boston Cooking-School Cook Book*. Boston: Little, Brown, and Company, 1896. Reprint, Mineola, NY: Dover Publications, Inc., 1997.

"Fashions in Calling Cards," *Harper's Bazar,* 1868. At: Victoriana.Com (see websites).

Fowler, Prof. O.S. "Posture and Kindred Signs Express Existing Sexual States," *Private Lectures on Perfect Men, Women and Children,* 1880. At: Victoriana.Com (see websites).

Garfield, Belle Mason. "Recipes out of the Past Belonging to Belle Mason Garfield and Her Mother, Caroline Robinson Mason." In *Mason Family Papers,* ms. 3254, container 1, folder 2. Cleveland, Ohio: The Western Reserve Historical Society Library.

Gillette, Mrs. F.L., and Hugo Ziemann. *The White House Cook Book*. Chicago: The Werner Company, 1887. Reprint, Ottenheimer Publications, 1999.

Harland, Marion. *Common Sense in the Household: A Manual of Practical Housewifery*. New York: Charles Scribner & Co., 1871.

Harper & Brothers, Publishers. "Cotton for Dresses," *Harper's New Monthly Magazine,* vol. XXXVI (December 1867–May 1868), 611-612. New York: Harper & Brothers, Publishers, 1868.

Harper & Brothers, Publishers. "Editor's Drawer," *Harper's New Monthly Magazine,* vol. XXXVI (December, 1867–May, 1868), 266, 673. New York: Harper & Brothers, Publishers, 1868.

Harper & Brothers, Publishers."Etiquette," *Harper's New Monthly Magazine,* vol. XXXVI (December 1867–May 1868), 384-387. New York: Harper & Brothers, Publishers, 1868.

Hartshorne, Henry, M.D. *The Household Cyclopedia of General Information Containing over Ten Thousand Receipts in All the Useful and Domestic Arts.* Philadelphia: T. Ellwood Zell and Pittsfield, MA: J. Brainard Clarke, 1871.

Hopley, Mrs. James R. "The Part Taken by Women in the History and Development of Ohio," Centennial Talk at Chillicothe, Ohio. Columbus, Ohio: Press of Fred J. Heer, May 20, 1903.

Huntington, Emily. *The Cooking Garden: A Systematized Course of Cooking for Pupils of All Ages, Including Plan of Work, Bills of Fare, Songs, and Letters of Information.* New York: Trow's Printing and Bookbinding Company, 1885.

Jeffries, Prof. B.G., and J.L. Nichols. *The Household Guide or Domestic Cyclopedia.* Naperville, IL: J.L. Nichols & Co., 1898.

Johnson, Helen Louise. *The Enterprising Housekeeper.* Philadelphia: The Enterprise Mfg. Co. of Pa., 1897.

Julius Ives & Co. *Catalogue.* New York, 1867.

Kirkpatrick, Mrs. T.J. *The Housekeepers New Cook Book.* Springfield, OH: Mast, Crowell & Kirkpatrick, 1883.

Klapthor, Margaret. *First Ladies Cook Book.* Parents' Magazine Press, 1969.

Ladies Association of The First Presbyterian Church. *The First Texas Cookbook.* Houston, TX: 1883. Reprint, *The First Texas Cookbook— A Thorough Treatise on the Art of Cookery in 1883.* Austin, TX: Eakin Publications, Inc., 1986.

Ladies of the M.E. Church. *Grayville Cook Book.* Grayville, IL: The Ladies of the M. E. Church, 1912.

Lincoln, Mrs. D.A. *Mrs. Lincoln's Boston Cook Book: What to Do and What Not to Do in Cooking.* Boston: Roberts Brothers, 1884. Reprint, *Boston*

Cooking School Cook Book—Mrs. D.A. Lincoln—A Reprint of the 1884 Classic. Mineola, NY: Dover, 1996.

Livingston, A.W. *Livingston and the Tomato.* Columbus, Ohio: A.W. Livingston's Sons, Seedmen, 1893. Reprint, with a foreword and appendix by Andrew F. Smith, Columbus: Ohio State University Press, 1998.

Mallon, Isabel A. "The Woman of Forty," *The Ladies' Home Journal,* vol. X, no. 10 (September 1893). At: the library of The Costume Gallery (see websites).

"Mourning and Funeral Usages." *Harper's Bazar,* April 17, 1886. At: Victoriana.Com (see websites).

"Our Country Friends," *The Lady's Friend,* May 1868. At: American Federation of Old West Re-enactors (see websites).

Phillips, Hazel Spencer. *The Golden Lamb.* Oxford, Ohio: The Oxford Press, 1993. At: Golden Lamb Website (see websites).

Plymouth Antiquarian Society. *The Plimoth Colony Cook Book.* Plymouth, MA: Plymouth Antiquarian Society, 1981.

Porter, Horace. "In Camp with U.S. Grant," *The Pittsburgh Bulletin.* April 27, 1901. At: Ulysses S. Grant Homepage (see websites).

"Practical Hints for the Household: The Amateur Housekeeper," *Godey's Lady's Book,* August, 1886. At: Victorian Women's World (see websites).

"Quotation by Worth." *Harper's Bazar,* December 15, 1877. At: Victoriana.Com (see websites).

Seely, Mrs. L. *Mrs. Seely's Cook Book: A Manual of French and American Cookery.* New York: The MacMillan Company, 1902.

Self-Help and Home-Study, vol. 1, no. 5. (January 1890). Boston: Seymour Eaton.

Stall, Sylvanus, D.D. *What a Young Man Ought to Know.* Philadelphia, PA: The Vir Publishing Company, 1904.

Stowe, Harriet Beecher. *House and Home Papers*. Boston: Fields, Osgood, & Co, 1869. At: Making of America (see websites).

Stratton, Florence. *Favorite Recipes of Famous Women*. New York: Harper, 1925.

The Picayune. *The Picayune's Creole Cook Book,* 2d ed. New Orleans, LA: The Picayune, 1901.

The Woman's Book, vol. 2. New York: Charles Scribner's Sons, 1894.

Tyree, Marion Cabell. *Housekeeping in Old Virginia.* Louisville, KY: John P. Morton & Co., 1879.

"Victorian Era Etiquette." At: Tamara's Victorian Corner (see websites).

Vincent, Marvin Richardson. *Amusement: A Force in Christian Training.* Troy, NY: W.H. Young, 1867. At: Making of America (see websites).

Wallace, Lily Haxworth. *The Rumford Complete Cook Book.* Providence, RI: Rumford Chemical Works, 1908.

West, Lucy Scott. *Journal account of stay at Rutherford White House, February 16–March 19, 1878.* At: Rutherford B. Hayes Presidential Center (see websites).

White, Mrs. Anna R. *Youth's Educator for Home and Society.* Chicago: Union Publishing House, 1896. At: Rochester History Department's Home Page: Youth's Educator for Home and Society (see websites).

Willard, Frances E. *A Wheel Within a Wheel: How I Learned to Ride the Bicycle (With Some Reflections by the Way).* Fleming H. Revell Co., 1895. Reprint, Bedford, MA: Applewood Books.

Women of the First Congregational Church of Marysville, Ohio. *Centennial Buckeye Cook Book.* Marysville, OH: J.H. Shearer & Son, 1876. Reprint, *Centennial Buckeye Cook Book Originally Published in 1876.* Columbus: Ohio State University Press, 2000.

Wright, A.S. *Wright's Book of 3,000 Practical Receipts.* New York: Dick & Fitzgerald, 1869. At: Making of America (see websites).

PAPERS AND MAGAZINES

19th Century Scientific American. At: 19th Century Scientific American Online (see websites).

Appletons Journal: A Magazine of General Literature. New York: D. Appleton and Company, 1869–1881. At: Making of America (see websites).

Godey's Lady's Book. At: Godey's Lady's Book On-Line and Godey's Archive: Home and Household Arts Archive (see websites).

Harper's Bazar. At: Victoriana.Com (see websites).

The Ohio Historical Society: Diary of Rutherford B. Hayes. At: The Ohio Historical Society (see websites).

The Ladies Home Journal. 1893–1895. At: the library of The Costume Gallery (see websites).

The Ladies Repository: A Monthly Periodical Devoted to Literature, Arts, and Religion. 1841–1876. At: Making of America (see websites).

WEBSITES

19th Century America   members.aol.com/Tchrfromoz/19thcent.html

19th Century American Literary, Historical, and Cultural Studies www.wsu.edu/~amerstu/19th/19th.html

19th Century Harpers Bazar Magazine www.victoriana.com/library/harpers/harpers.html

19th Century Scientific American Online www.history.rochester.edu/Scientific_American

American Federation of Old West Reenactors   www.afowr.com

American Memory: Historical Collections for the National Digital Library memory.loc.gov/ammem/amhome.html

American Women's History: A Guide to Resources and Research on the Web   web.uccs.edu/~history/index/women.html#home

The Costume Gallery   www.costumegallery.com

Godey's Archive: Home and Household Arts Archive www.spiritone.com/~zsk/hartarch.htm

Godey's Ladies Book On-Line   www.history.rochester.edu/godeys

Golden Lamb Website   www.maisonettegroup.com/golden-lamb

The Household Cyclopedia   members.nbci.com/mspong/contents.html

Internet Modern History Sourcebook
   www.fordham.edu/halsall/mod/modsbook.html

Making of America Project   moa.umdl.umich.edu or
   moa.cit.cornell.edu/moa

Matilda Joslyn Gage Website: Links to Websites on Women in the 19th
   Century   www.pinn.net/~sunshine/gage/features/gage_lnk.html

Miss Abigail's Time Warp Advice: Old Advice for Contemporary
   Dilemmas   www.missabigail.com

The Ohio Hisotrical Society   www.ohiohistory.org

Pilgrim New Media   www.plgrm.com

Rochester History Department's Home Page. Youth's Educator for Home
   and Society   www.history.rochester.edu/ehp-book/yefhas

Rutgers University Library: Nineteenth Century
   www.libraries.rutgers.edu/rul/rr_gateway/research_guides/history/
   texts_by_period.shtml#19c1800s

Rutherford B. Hayes Presidential Center   www.rbhayes.org

Tamara's Victorian Corner   www.geocities.com/Paris/Opera/1829/ettiquette

Ulysses S. Grant Homepage   www.mscomm.com/~ulysses

Victorian Women's World   www.spiritone.com/~zsk

Victorian Women Writers Project   www.indiana.edu/~letrs/vwwp

Victoriana.com   www.victoriana.com

The Walter H. & Leonore Annenberg Rare Book & Manuscript
   Library of the University of Pennsylvania. *Household Words: Women
   Write for and from the Kitchen.*
   www.library.upenn.edu/special/gallery/aresty/aresty22.html

 INDEX